D1329723

POWER, PASSION, AND *Faith*

Emmy Carlsson Evald

Suffragist and Social Activist

Sharon M. Wyman

Open Books Press
Saint Louis, Missouri

Copyright © 2022 Sharon M. Wyman

All rights reserved. No part of this book may be reproduced
or transmitted in any form or by any means, electronic or
mechanical, including photocopying, recording, or by any
information storage and retrieval system, without permission in
writing from the publisher.

Published by Open Books Press, USA

www.OpenBooksPress.com
info@OpenBooksPress.com

An imprint of Pen & Publish, LLC
www.PenandPublish.com
Saint Louis, Missouri
(314) 827-6567

Print ISBN: 978-1-941799-95-6
eBook ISBN: 978-0-9779530-5-9

Library of Congress Control Number: 202194406

For all the saints

"And when the chief shepherd appears,
you will win the crown of glory that never fades away."

—1 Peter 5:4 (NRSV)

Contents

Acknowledgments

Many hands have contributed to the writing of this biography among them were friends and family members, who encouraged me along my journey. I am especially grateful to my husband, Bob Wyman, who kept the faith; to my sister, Susan Evans, for her technical assistance; and to my mother, Emmy Carlson Merritt, who kept the story alive.

I also owe a debt of gratitude to librarians and the ELCA archivists, who pulled volumes of materials for me to peruse week after week; and to the families who stored boxes of Emmy's personal papers, often tied with pink ribbons, and typed on onion skin, waiting to be discovered; and to my publisher, Jennifer Geist, who made all things possible.

Thanks to you all.

Sharon M. Wyman

Prologue

Warm, pungent odors rise from the subway grates as panel trucks rattle down the street en route to their next delivery. New York City is just beginning to stir on July 1, 1938; for Emmy, it is a day of reckoning.

Emmy has championed women's causes from social justice to women's suffrage throughout her life. But her crowning achievement, as president of the Woman's Missionary Society, is the Lutheran Home for Women. The home was a financial success due to Emmy's hard work, boundless energy, and innate business sense.

But over the years, her well-proportioned body has grown thin, and wisps of wayward gray hairs radiate from her face. Still, beneath her wiry frame is a woman of strength and determination, which often results in an authoritarian management style. She is a mover and a shaker—an unstoppable force.

Her faith is strong and her will impervious to changes within the Woman's Missionary Society. Now after decades of personal sacrifice, the powers that be wanted to boot her out . . . to remove her forever from her life's work.

At age eighty, she awaits a confrontation with the women she once led.

Introduction

The Swedish Exodus

Sweeping reforms awakened the Swedes to fresh possibilities and a desire to begin anew. They began fleeing their homeland in the mid-1800s for a variety of reasons: a fresh start, religious freedom, or a sense of adventure. Over the years, more than one million would arrive on the shores of the United States. So much so, that by the early twentieth century, nearly one-fifth of all the people born in Sweden were living in America.[1]

Most of the early emigrants came from rural areas, outnumbering those from the city five to one.[2] Many came from Småland, a southern province in Sweden, where farming was the primary occupation. Today the region is known for fine crystal, Pippi Longstocking, and Ikea. But before that, not much had changed in Sweden since the Middle Ages. People lived in small villages and shared pastureland and fields. Rolling hills, deep forests, pristine lakes, and an abundance of moose filled the countryside. Simple red-frame homes and stone walls lined the streets. Churches with onion-shaped steeples and arched windows beckoned parishioners to worship. Farmers tilled rock-filled fields and tended a few milk cows but had only a trifle to show for their work.

Their diets—largely vegetarian—consisted of barley mush and potatoes along with some salt herring and *skanning* (fermented sour milk). Due to the compulsory education system, most could read and write, but this did not protect them from Sweden's economic, political, and social changes.

Traditionally, farmers had large families to ensure a ready labor force. Plots of land customarily passed down from fathers to sons. Now that Sweden lived peacefully with its neighbors, sons no longer headed off to war. This, coupled with recent vaccinations and other medical advances, caused the population to nearly double between 1810 and 1850. As plots of land grew smaller, less acreage meant fewer crops to feed their families. Siblings worked as sharecroppers or as hired hands for low wages. When the potato crop failed in the 1860s, famine beset the nation.[3]

The government struggled to meet the needs of the people; overwhelmed by the population explosion, inadequate health care resulted. The Industrial Revolution, which had overtaken Europe and the United States, failed to reach Sweden. Given the scarcity of jobs, unemployment rose. Land-poor Swedes fell into the lower classes with little hope for their future.[4]

* * * *

Religious freedom also contributed to the mass exodus of Swedish emigrants. The spiritual revival, known as the "Lasare" movement, created a stir within the Lutheran Church, the state church of Sweden. The Pietism (from the word *piety*) movement grew popular in the eighteenth century.[5] The Lasares focused on a more personal and spiritual worship experience and endorsed the temperance movement.

Emmy's father, Rev. Erland Carlsson, lived in the province of Småland in the heart of the movement where he held gatherings in private homes for Bible studies and prayer meetings. Once an illegal practice, such meetings were now lawful, but not sanctioned by the church. As government employees, pastors, tangled in red tape, had little time to shepherd their flocks. Eager to break the bonds of the state-run church, they, along with groups of their parishioners, set sail for America.[6]

Rev. Eric Janson arrived first. He emigrated from his home in the mid-1840s with a group of fifteen hundred followers known as Jansonites.[7] Many of the emigrants died of cholera aboard the ship. The remainder settled in Bishop Hill, Illinois, the "New Jerusalem," and lived within a communal setting. Janson's followers considered him a harsh and controlling leader. After his murder in 1850, the colony fell into decline.[8]

Rev. Lars Paul Esbjörn, a self-righteous man of deep conviction, came in 1849 with a band of 146 that settled in Andover in western Illinois. Once established, he invited his friends to join him in America. The first pastor to answer Esbjörn's call was Rev. Tuve Nilson Hasselquist, an advocate of the Lasare movement.[9] Emmy's father, whose opportunities in Sweden had dwindled due to his outspokenness, responded next. Erland arrived in 1853 and settled in Chicago. His two colleagues, Rev. Jonas Swensson and Rev. Olaf Andren, followed in 1856. These five pioneer pastors—Esbjörn, Hasselquist, Carlsson, Swensson, and Andren—formed the Augustana Lutheran Synod, whose basic tenets are still a part of the Evangelical Lutheran Church in America.[10]

* * * *

Immigration agents, or "runners," hired by the American shipping lines, railroads, and land companies, promoted fresh opportunities in America adding to the flurry of immigrants.[11] The *Hemlandet* newspaper, printed in Chicago, featured glowing accounts of life in America, intensifying the desire to leave Sweden. Emmy's father wrote articles for the paper and a guidebook on immigration. Because the Swedes were acquainted with his name, multitudes followed him to Chicago.

Encouraged by recent accounts from America, emigrants, their hearts a flutter, headed for a home across the sea to *framtidslandet*—the land of the future. Some sold their farms; others abandoned their homes, leaving the family farm untended. While many sailed for America, others stayed and sent their children, not knowing if they would see them again, if they even survived the sea voyage. Still others sailed for America against their parents' wishes, clutching their dismissal papers from the Lutheran Church in Sweden, their belongings packed in wooden chests.

The earliest emigrants departed from Gothenburg, Sweden, for the port cities of Hull or Liverpool, England. Others followed a route from Hamburg, Germany.[12]

They traveled cheaply in the steerage section or the lowest deck of the ship. Squashed like cattle, they endured dank air and dark, cramped quarters. Common sleeping areas offered the passengers little privacy. Their voyage meant endless days at sea staring at a blue horizon and rolling waves. Aboard the ship, sickness, disease, and boredom consumed the weary travelers. Shipping lines offered free meals of beef, porridge, and dried fruit. But the emigrants found the food unfamiliar and often unfit to eat, preferring baskets of hardtack and dried meat for the journey.[13]

During the ocean crossing on the *St. Patrick*, Emmy's father urged travelers to stay active—to avoid the monotony of the voyage and seasickness—and to bring a few good Swedish books. He advised other passengers to ". . . stay out of bed and in motion, promenade the deck, work the pump, and be busy with sewing, crocheting, and whatever else one can do. This contributes to health and comfort."[14]

In doing so, the Swedes kept their minds and their bodies strong for the ordeals to come. Upon landing at Castle Garden, the center for immigration in New York City, arrivals were met with thievery and chicanery. Unable to speak the language and unfamiliar with American currency, they appeared easy prey for unsavory characters.[15] (After 1890, immigrants were processed through Ellis Island.)

Once the American frontier expanded past the Appalachian Mountains into the upper Mississippi Valley and the Midwestern plains, people headed west. Soon the fertile farmlands of Illinois, Wisconsin, Iowa, and Minnesota developed as the center of Scandinavian immigration. Often the immigrants settled together, forming Swedish colonies or "little Swedens," such as those in Lindsborg, Kansas, and Chisago Lake, Minnesota. They worshipped together and held to their Swedish traditions.

Once completed, the Erie Canal connected the Hudson River with the Great Lakes and made Chicago the destination of choice for many Swedish immigrants. They made their way westward on paddle steamers and canal boats pulled by a team of oxen and settled along the north branch of the Chicago River atop marshy swamplands.

The locals, who thought recent arrivals carried diseases, did not extend a warm welcome. Such was the case for a party from

Västergötland, Sweden, who arrived in Chicago during the summer of 1852 and set forth by boat to Sheboygan, Michigan. The men ventured into town for information, leaving the women, one of whom was possibly Emmy's mother, and children behind with their belongings. Unable to locate anybody who understood Swedish in the small town, the men returned to the dock and waited with the other travelers who rested helpless and hungry atop their luggage. When the boat from Chicago returned after a few days, the group got aboard and headed back to the city.[16]

* * * *

Although incorporated in 1837, the city of Chicago, with its miles of mud, resembled that of a burgeoning frontier town along Lake Michigan. Writer John Peyton once described Chicago as "the city situated on both sides of the Chicago River . . . a sluggish, slimy stream too lazy to clean itself."[17]

In the 1850s, Swedish activist Fredricka Bremer concluded that Chicago was not fit for folks to live or work, claiming it was "one of the most miserable and ugly cities which I have yet seen in America."[18] However, she found the people to be "most agreeable and delightful."[19]

Piles of garbage and industrial refuse, human waste, and animal droppings spilled into the city streets. Unpaved roads were littered with tree stumps and some standing trees. Dead animals lined the ditches, and wild pigs ran rampant through the streets. Foul odors rose from raw sewage, and debris floated down the Chicago River, dumping sewage and waste into Lake Michigan.

Sidewalks were nonexistent, and the water supply was contaminated. Buildings dotted the landscape. Lumber yards, commercial entities, and wharves marked the lakefront, and the city air reeked from the meat-packing houses. Railroad tracks spread outward from the town resembling spokes on a wheel and transported everything from immigrants to carloads of beef, pork, lumber, and grain.

Transportation was by horseback or stagecoach, which jostled passengers, bumping them to and fro. When the rains came, the roads were impassable. Horse-drawn wagons mired in bottomless mud holes. Other roads, which were constructed from timbers or planks, were known as "corduroy roads" because they resembled the fabric. These allowed vehicles to travel more easily. Even so, buggies rattled over wooden planks, spraying unsuspecting pedestrians with dirt and debris.[20]

Hot summer winds blew puffs of dust into the air, and soot billowed from the smokestacks of passing trains, covering the town with black grit. Dark clouds of industrial pollution hung in the air.[21] The bitterly cold winters lasted an eternity. Before the spring thaw, ice chunks floated along the lakefront.

City folk lived in marshy swamp areas where brackish water pooled and snakes gathered. Standing water filled with filth led to disease—cholera, tuberculosis, and typhoid among the deadliest.[22] Amid the mud and ooze lurked other creepy-crawly vermin slithering in the muck. During the worst of times, the immigrants clung to their faith, which promised them a better life in heaven.

Outside of town, prairie grass grew eight to ten feet tall, offering little protection for the settlers. With its thick roots deeply matted into the ground, this "inland ocean" formed a sea of grass that rippled like water. The fertile land and trees provided raw materials for fuel, buildings, and fences, or lumber, which could be sold. But working the land with wooden plows and a horse—or even a man—made farming difficult.

The landscape began to change with innovations such as the steel-edged plow designed by Cyrus McCormick, which allowed farmers to clear the land, cracking through the grass roots with a team of oxen. Sodbusting opened the prairie to human cultivation. The newly opened board of trade in Chicago enabled farmers to bring their grain crops to be graded and stored, eventually creating a futures market. Grain elevators stimulated farming and can still be seen along the railways, standing tall against the Midwestern landscape.

Word of a railroad connecting Chicago to major cities such as St. Louis spread throughout the city. Completed in 1856, the Illinois Central, a massive venture with more than seven hundred miles of track, linked the northern and southern portions of Illinois. This iron horse did not freeze like the Mississippi River in the harsh winters, allowing heavy cargo to move back and forth regardless of the weather. The pattern of commerce in the Midwest changed forever in the process.

Entrepreneurs saw potential for economic growth, and with it, opportunities for wealth, resulting in a steady stream of speculators to the area. Among them were men such as Marshall Field, who hoped to find a job as a respectable mercantile clerk in a dry goods store. Rand McNally started a mapping and printing business. Philip Armour's meat-packing enterprise and Gustavus Swift's stockyards came to be the centerpiece of Chicago's economy through the rest of the nineteenth century and into the twentieth century.

By 1857 Chicago was one of the largest cities in the nation with a population of thirty thousand residents.[23] Before long, an explosion of settlements could be found in northern and central Illinois. The number of Swedes far outpaced those from other Scandinavian countries. By the 1860s, Chicago was the center of Swedish America and its cultural identity.

The Swedes brought their expertise and abilities to Chicago, where they found both skilled and unskilled job opportunities. Most men worked in trades such as carpentry, cabinetmaking, blacksmithing, and construction. Swedish women used their domestic proficiency as seamstresses or servants—jobs requiring little English.[24]

The early settlers established Swedish communities and churches, solidifying the area's vibrant culture. Swedish schools and hospitals unified the settlers and attracted other immigrants to Chicago. Emmy's family resided in one of the largest of these neighborhoods, known as Swede Town.[25]

Bound by Chicago Avenue and Market, Oak, and Larrabee Streets, Swede Town, located in one of the worst sections of the city, lacked sanitation. Rows of wooden shanties speckled with mud lined the streets. Candles were used for light.[26] Paper pulled tautly against the windows kept the cold Chicago winds at bay.

Given their low wages, the Swedes looked for inexpensive housing near their jobs. They could ill afford public transportation and needed to be within walking distance of their work.[27] Wooden city buildings provided them with ample opportunities to use their carpentry skills. Other amenities, such as restaurants, boarding houses, social clubs, and shops, were within easy reach of the residents.

Emmy's father planted the seeds of a Swedish Lutheran church within the community. His small congregation found the sights and sounds of America unfamiliar. Coming from the "Land of the Midnight Sun," where summer meant twenty-four hours of daylight and winter brought months of darkness, the environment seemed as strange as the language. Yet despite their poverty and other hardships, church members worked to build a better way of life for future generations of faith.

Chapter One

The Early Years in America (1853–1875)

Emmy Carlsson Evald was a woman of courage, a crusader for equal rights, and according to friends, "a force to be reckoned with." Her story begins in Sweden with her father, Rev. Dr. Erland Carlsson, who endowed her with two guiding principles: a proud Swedish history and an abiding faith. Born on August 22, 1822, Erland grew up in Älghult Parish, an impoverished farming community in Småland in southern Sweden. Having lost his father at an early age, he worked hard to achieve an education at Lund University.

As a pastor, young Erland's liberal viewpoints often conflicted with the state-run Lutheran Church of Sweden. In addition, his long but artful sermons annoyed the local bishop, further limiting his options.

Meanwhile, in America, trouble brewed in Chicago. Local pastors worried about the Swedes and their increased use of alcohol. More troublesome, Methodists were coming to town,[1] whose ideology differed from the Lutherans in that Southern Methodist churches tended to accept slaveholders. The church polity was also dissimilar.[2]

Consequently, they asked Erland to join them with hopes of establishing a Swedish Lutheran church in Chicago. Given his dim job prospects in Sweden, Erland agreed and left his homeland of pink and purple lupine on June 3, 1853. His decision begat generations of Americans with Swedish ancestry.

Erland, along with 176 other emigrants, journeyed first to Hamburg, Germany, and then to Liverpool, England. From there the group embarked on the *St. Patrick* bound for America. To stay active, travelers participated in Bible classes and hymn singing (often accompanied by Erland on his violin), and when possible, studied English vocabulary and grammar.[3]

Erland arrived in Chicago on August 28, 1853, at the age of thirty-one. Luckily, he found lodging in an attic room with an outdoor staircase. Board and laundry cost ten dollars per month. He took responsibility for the room's upkeep and his stove.

His first months in a strange city proved particularly harsh and not very encouraging.

> His first Christmas Eve, he had been out inviting people to a *Julotta* [a Christmas morning worship service]. He came home all alone to his attic room. It was bitterly cold and there was no fire in the little stove. When he went to wash his hands, the water was frozen, the pitcher fell on the floor and cracked into pieces. That was too much for the lonesome, homesick pastor and he sat down and cried bitterly. Far away from his loved ones . . .
>
> —Emmy Evald[4]

Most immigrants faced a period of adjustment; as a new pastor, Erland carried an extra burden: that of building a church. Part of his would-be flock had affiliated with different congregations. Others had simply drifted away from church or Chicago altogether. Thirty-six remained, including eight married couples and twenty singletons, one of whom would become his wife and Emmy's mother.

Erland's first church was housed in a Norwegian Lutheran church at the corner of Superior and Orleans Streets. Once the wee congregation could afford a church of their own, the parishioners purchased a church building and the adjoining empty lot for less than $2,500 in October 1854.[5] They called the church the Swedish Evangelical Lutheran Church of Chicago, forming the only Swedish Lutheran church in the city. (The name changed to the Swedish Evangelical Lutheran Immanuel Church of Chicago. Immanuel, meaning "God with us," became its corporate name. The word "Swedish" was later deleted from the name.)

A white picket fence surrounded the wooden church with its tall spire, and an open door welcomed parishioners. The church, referred to as Immanuel Lutheran, marked a beginning for the immigrants whose courage and aspirations laid the groundwork for the Christian community.

A skilled organizer, Erland and his fellow Lutheran pastors formed the Augustana Synod, which required extensive travel throughout the Midwest. He soon emerged as a central figure in church development, mission, and education, crisscrossing the country. As an adult, Emmy would follow in his footsteps.

For the Swedes, the church represented both a social and spiritual connection, and membership was a status symbol. To "belong" to the church where a well-regarded pastor preached meant an everyday laborer could attain a level of respectability.[6] The church was the center of community life with fairs and picnics—the "tie that binds."[7] Within the community, folks compared church attendance to good citizenship, like paying taxes and voting.[8]

Emmy's father toiled endlessly on behalf of his growing congregation, serving his flock as a counselor, a realtor, a translator, and—at times—a mailman. Long lines of parishioners, seeking aid, formed outside his attic room causing his landlord, who tired of the commotion, to evict him. Deadly cholera swept through Chicago in the fall of 1854. Due to malnutrition, many immigrants literally died in the street on their way to work and were loaded onto wagons for burial. Surrounded by the acrid smell of death, Erland tended his parishioners as best he could, contracting a mild case of the disease himself, which would later manifest itself in bouts of ill health throughout Emmy's life. Ten percent of church members perished that year.[9] In all, Erland estimated that nearly 60 percent of the Swedish immigrants who arrived in Chicago that fall succumbed to the disease.[10]

* * * *

Thanks to a common language and shared faith, Swedes often married each other. Erland, too, proposed to a member of his flock. He and his bride, Eva Charlotta Anderson, wed in a quiet ceremony on May 25, 1855. Eva was twenty-six and Erland thirty-three. His sculpted forehead and deep-set eyes accentuated his boyish good looks. Chin whiskers made him appear older than his years.

With her chestnut hair pulled tautly into a bun, Eva, on the other hand, looked as plain as prairie grass, although the curl of her smile softened her stern countenance. Those who knew her thought her to be a humble Christian woman with a pleasing personality whose life encompassed good deeds. She nursed the sick, cared for the homeless, and was a wise, tender mother and an exemplary pastor's wife, who had time for everyone and was friendly toward all.[11]

Little is known about Eva's early childhood. She was born on March 11, 1829, the daughter of Mr. and Mrs. Anders Anderson of Timmele Parish, in Västergötland, Sweden. Exactly when the family arrived in America is unclear. Multiple sources cite various dates ranging from 1847 to 1852.

The Anderson family may have been part of a Västergötland group who came to America and proceeded to Sheboygan, Michigan, only to be stranded on the pier unable to communicate with the residents. One account indicates Mr. Anderson was a blacksmith and wagon maker who immigrated to Taylor Falls, Minnesota, and subsequently to St. Charles, Illinois, before moving to Chicago. Church records show that the Anderson family arrived in the city in 1851.

* * * *

The financial crisis of 1857 caused bank failures and unemployment unlike any the country had experienced. In Chicago, families evacuated from the city proper and wandered into the countryside where they tried to sustain themselves on potatoes and corn. Men worked for fifty cents a day to provide for their families, and women took in laundry to make ends meet. Landlords charged twenty dollars per month for rent and flour rose to a costly seven dollars a barrel. Rumors of muskrat skins being used in lieu of cash could be heard along city streets.[12]

That same year, Erland, weary and in declining health, resettled his family in Geneva, Illinois, a sleepy little hamlet on the fringes of Chicago. He organized a Lutheran church in town and hoped to rest. There, on September 18, 1857, Emmy, baptized Emlie Christina, came into the world. She was the second child to bless the Carlsson home; Emmy's sister, Annie, had been born the previous year. Nobody imagined the woman she would turn out to be, the influence she would wield, or the respect she would gain.

In less than a year, the family returned to their home in Chicago, where Erland continued to serve Immanuel Lutheran Church and the family grew. Ebenezer arrived April 1859 and Samuel in February 1864. Between 1868 and 1872, Emmy's mother gave birth to four more children. Although little Ester lived for two years, the other children died during infancy. All in all, the Carlssons buried more than half of their children, which was common for the time. Because infants often perished within days of their birth, families sometimes waited several months before naming them. Emmy's brother Sam appeared so frail his parents held a baptism the day he was born.

* * * *

Prayer meetings at the family home were so popular that the parsonage filled to overflowing. On occasion, smoky oil lamps and flaming candles absorbed the oxygen, making it difficult for the worshippers to breathe.[13] The Carlssons also appreciated the arts and music. Erland played both the violin and the flute, and friends recollected a house filled with joy.

Days were never idle during the early years of the church. Recalling their own plight as immigrants facing hunger and disease, the family focused on mission projects within the church. Their home at 151 Lincoln Avenue served as a refuge for the homeless and a hospital for the sick. At various times, as many as sixty immigrants lived with the family. One family friend referred to their home as a "little Castle Garden" after the central immigration station in New York City.[14] Their home at Lincoln and Cleveland Avenue was used as temporary housing for Augustana Hospital. Emmy's parents eventually sold their property to the hospital in 1886, donating a portion of the proceeds to the organization.

With all the comings and goings, a youthful Emmy occasionally misinterpreted what she saw, especially when needy families arrived on the Carlssons' doorstep.

We had no immigrant home. The church served as such and they slept in the pews. As a child, I remember Mother kneeling as a nurse cleaning the sores of a poor immigrant's legs infected and full of worms.

I have seen her carrying out big kettles of meatball soup with potatoes and carrots to the hungry, poor, and penniless immigrants in our backyard. As children, we used to go up and down the aisles of the church looking at the immigrants and feeling so sorry that Mother and Father came from such people.

—Emmy Evald[15]

Emmy eventually realized that the poor people in the pews did not represent all Swedes but reflected her father's Christian love and the urgent need for immigrant aid.[16]

* * * *

Once the Swedes were settled and the church building constructed, the congregation made plans for a school. They erected a two-story building on an empty lot adjacent to the church. In addition, the need for reading materials and devotional books outpaced the supply brought from Sweden. To remedy the problem, the upper floor of the building housed the first business office of the Swedish Lutheran Publication Society. Smelling of paper and ink, the society, started in January 1855, published the New Testament and other books in Swedish.

The publication society also printed the *Hemlandet* ("Homeland") newspaper, which reported on social and political issues, such as slavery and temperance. Emmy's father promoted the paper, which reminded readers to stay true to their Lutheran upbringing. The venture proved rewarding for young Emmy and her siblings, who earned a few pennies each for folding the paper with newsprint-stained hands.[17]

In the summer, classrooms occupied the main floor of the frame building. Emmy and her siblings attended "Swede school" in their formative years. As students, they learned Swedish, scriptures, and the catechism corresponding to today's parochial schools. The curriculum for children and adults included English, although, in the home, they communicated in Swedish. Off and on, immigrants also resided in the schoolhouse.

As religious leader, Erland's responsibilities went beyond Sunday worship services. He and his fellow pastors sought to recruit and educate students who would actively minister to the growing needs of rural communities. Although a theological degree was not necessary to pursue a calling in the ministry, most denominations, despite being strapped for cash, built seminaries to inspire young men to further their religious education.[18]

As a result, the schoolhouse played a different role from 1860 to 1863 as the first home of a newly established school, Augustana College and Theological Seminary. The lower floor of the schoolhouse served as a lecture hall and the upper floor as a dormitory. The students were poor but suffered no want.[19] Profits from the *Hemlandet* helped to defray the cost of the college.

Wide-eyed and inquisitive, Emmy mistakenly observed the students at the college. "As children, we thought it was awfully funny that these big men had to go to school where we had learned our ABCs," she said.[20] Of course, the students focused on preaching, not reading and writing.

The women of Immanuel Lutheran Church also involved themselves in the college. Ready-made bed linens were unavailable in the mid-1800s. Emmy's mother's sewing society chatted over coffee as nimble fingers worked to make sheets, pillowcases, and towels and construct quilts and mattresses for the beds at the seminary. The mattresses, filled with crunchy corn husks, made for a lumpy night's sleep.

In addition, the women's group prepared the dormitories for the seminary students by cleaning and scrubbing the rooms. They made beds and washed and ironed the students' laundry. Without a dining room, church families invited the students to their homes for meals.

Emmy's fond childhood memories included the early days of the seminary and college. With chores to be done, beds to be made, and meals to prepare, her little hands helped where they could. Wearing a simple calico dress, she headed to the dormitory with slips of paper telling the students where to go for their meals. "There was one cranky student and no home wanted to feed him," said Emmy. "He came and complained to Father. Father told him, 'It is no wonder, when [at dinner] you asked, '*Duger detta att ata?*' . . . 'What is this?'"[21] The story provided a lesson on gratitude and manners.

* * * *

As Emmy grew, so did Chicago. Its population now outpaced St. Louis and Cincinnati. Most businesses located by the Chicago River along Wacker Drive and Lake Street, making downtown a central area for shopping and financial transactions.

On the political front, President James Buchanan occupied the White House, and the country teetered on the brink of war. As one of the nation's largest states, Illinois was a swing state, with nearly one-fourth of its population foreign born. The rural communities of southern Illinois supported proslavery views and the northern portion of the state pro-Union, having been inhabited by Union sympathizers from the Northeast. In 1860, Abraham Lincoln won the Republican Party's nomination at the Wigwam convention center in Chicago, putting the city on the map.

Emmy was almost four when the Confederates attacked Fort Sumter, signaling the start of the Civil War. As the war broke out, antislavery ideology had a firm foothold on the city, and the economy boomed. Northern states prospered with increases in commodities and wages. Swedish immigrants—still troubled by famine and unemployment in their homeland—continued to flock to Chicago in search of a better life, making Chicago the largest cluster of Swedes in the United States.[22]

In those days, all good citizens did their patriotic duty. Many young men from Immanuel Lutheran Church served under the Union "colors,"[23] having aligned themselves with the antislavery stance of their mother country. The times were not conducive for a growing college, however. As more men marched off to war, enrollments at Augustana College and Theological Seminary declined. In 1863, after much discussion, the college moved from the schoolhouse behind the Superior Street church and relocated south of the city in Paxton, Illinois, surrounded by fertile farmland.

Not everyone agreed with the move, but Erland and other pastors hoped the locale near the Illinois Central Railroad would bring students to Augustana and that the community would assist the college and help it grow. Instead, the flood of immigrants headed north to Minnesota and west toward Nebraska and Kansas. Meanwhile, the war dominated the news.

As a socially minded Republican, Erland endorsed President Lincoln. In April 1865, when word spread of President Lincoln's assassination by John Wilkes Booth, Emmy found her father sitting at the kitchen table with his head bowed and his shoulders shaking as he sobbed. Stunned by what she saw and unable to imagine an event that would cause her father such sorrow, she assumed the worst . . . God must have died.

After two weeks, the body of the fallen president lay in state at the Old Court House in Courthouse Square at the corners of Randolph, Clark, LaSalle, and Washington Streets. As the draped funeral train passed carrying Lincoln's body, Erland hoisted Emmy's brother Eben onto his shoulders to watch history in the making. The Prairie State would bury its native son in Springfield.

After the Civil War, many veterans returned to the city. Some arrived by train, some by horseback, and others came on foot. Keen to rebuild their lives and in search of family members, they returned to Chicago. Battered by disease and alcoholism, wounded, maimed, and on makeshift crutches, the soldiers found a haven in the churchyard where they lay strewn across the lawn, their uniforms tattered and torn. Having seen the horrors of war, the battle-weary men found eight-year-old Emmy scampering about to be a welcome sight. She and her mother brought steaming pots of meaty broth and vegetables to the ailing and exhausted men and bound their wounds.

When General William T. Sherman arrived in Chicago to review the impoverished troops and offer his assistance, he spotted Emmy in the yard. He kissed her hand in gratitude for her kindness to others and her service to the troops, his scruffy whiskers brushing her skin. She never forgot the gesture. His thankfulness was the first of many accolades she would receive.

Emmy witnessed huge changes in the city during its industrial era. By the mid-nineteenth century, railroads converged in Chicago, bringing with them prosperity. The city became known for steel manufacturing, technology, and refinement. On the international scene, Chicago was the center for meat packing with its stockyards and processing capabilities.

Speculators learned, if they guessed right, that they could make big money. Dollars flowed through Chicago's marketplace and were reinvested in areas such as banking and finance. Chicago expanded into a hot spot for investing and speculation and a mecca for immigrants with modern ideas. High rollers lived at the top of the food chain with those in desperate poverty at the bottom.

A restored Union brought changes in merchandising and packaging. Folks could now buy Pillsbury flour and wash with Ivory soap or soothe their aching heads with Bayer aspirin. But as the nation's economy soared, disaster loomed for the Carlsson family and the city of Chicago.

* * * *

Within five years, the membership at Immanuel Lutheran Church had jumped from 220 in 1860 to 525 in 1865. Parishioners squeezed shoulder to shoulder into hard-backed pews. The stuffy quarters caused some churchgoers to swoon from the heat. Because the small wooden church housed only one-half of the congregation, members elected to purchase property at 218 Sedgwick Street for $7,000 in 1867 (some church records indicate the purchase price was $8,500),[24] and plans got underway to build a different church.

In November 1869, the congregation held a farewell service at the Superior Street church, after which Erland and the deacons carried the communion vessels and the church Bible to the church at Sedgwick and Hobbie Streets.[25] Moving so far north concerned a few parishioners. But the area known as Swede Town, too, had expanded with nearly five thousand residents bounded by Division, Superior, Franklin, and Larrabee Streets and the north branch of the Chicago River.[26] Of course, they could not foresee the events that would befall the city in October 1871.

The church sanctuary proved to be the grandest of its day. The spire with its gilded cross rose 154 feet toward heaven and the building cost a whopping $34,000. Everything looked promising, and the congregation happily anticipated the future. However, the church still owed more than $22,000 on the property, which worried church members, and they took steps to reduce the debt. They planned a special meeting for October 9, 1871, but it never occurred.[27]

The autumn day appeared ordinary. Swing bridges shifted back and forth across the river at Rush and State Streets to allow schooners to enter the city with deliveries and consumer goods. Horsedrawn carriages and wagons bustled up and down Wells Street. That evening, a blaze of orange appeared on the horizon.

Fire alarms did not phase the city's residents even with the recent drought. Not to mention, Chicago sidewalks and bridges were made of wood, and many of the houses had flammable roofs of pine and tar, plus bales of hay and straw filled local barns. Folks assumed the river would stop the flames and contain any fire. They were wrong.

The blaze broke out around half past eight in the evening on October 8, near Mrs. O'Leary's barn at the rear of 137 DeKoven Street where she stabled her milk cows. High winds whipped the fire out of control. Flames flew across the river, sending onlookers fleeing for their lives.

Emmy's father preached that Sunday at the Evensong service, a choral worship service combining vespers and evening prayers. Scripture readings and music made up much of the spiritual observance. On his way home, Erland noticed a reddish color in the sky to the south.

> The fire was more than three English miles from Immanuel Lutheran Church, and no one feared any danger. But before sunrise the following morning, most of Chicago was in ashes. Early Monday morning the fire flashed across the river to the north

side where the ravaging element like an ocean of fire spread out from the river to the lake and soon swept everything in its path.

—Erland Carlsson[28]

The Great Chicago Fire of 1871 would change the course of history for the Carlsson daughters and Immanuel Lutheran Church. However, at the time of the fire, Emmy and Annie were out of the country. Having completed their public education in Chicago, the teenagers were safe and sound in Kalmar, Sweden, at the Rostad School for Girls. Under the guidance of *Mamsell* Cecill Fryxell, the Carlsson daughters busied themselves with their academics and training in Christian virtues. Letters from home told of the fire and the toll it took on the family, the church, and the city itself.

The Swedes bore the brunt of the disaster more than any other ethnic group. The latter resided in neighborhoods throughout the city, whereas approximately two-thirds of the Swedes lived in Swede Town, which had been in the direct path of the fire.[29] The neighborhood ignited tantamount to a tinder box, reducing the entire North Side to ashes. Grabbing whatever personal possessions they could snatch from the flames, families abandoned their homes for safer ground.

The same bell that had tolled for President Lincoln rang out until the courthouse, consumed with fire, crumbled to the ground. Hundreds of homes in the city and four Swedish churches fell into a pile of rubble.

Erland and Eva watched in horror and church members wept as flames crackled about the church and rafters crashed to the ground in a fiery rage. Only the church records could be saved. Fire also destroyed the congregation's first church on Superior Street. When it was over, nine out of every ten church members, including the Carlssons and their two young sons, Eben (age twelve) and Sam (age seven), were homeless.[30]

The loss was devastating for Emmy's family who lost their home, valued at $25,000 in the 1870 Census, and their personal property, assessed at $1,000. Fortunately, the Carlssons found lodging with friends. Others slept in open fields away from the scorched earth. People lost everything—their homes, their church, and their belongings. But not one church member died in the conflagration.[31]

The fire turned the tide for the city. All total, one-third of the city's residents remained homeless with 18,000 buildings burned and more than $199 million in property damage. Roughly fifty insurance companies went belly-up because of the fire, which meant insurance claims went unpaid. The destruction would become the yardstick by which future fires were measured.

Chicago businesses sold everything but commemorative T-shirts. Locals tried to sell what housewares they had to restart their lives elsewhere. Frantic construction began. Buildings grander than before rose from the ashes, and city leaders established stricter fire codes.

After the blaze, church members met to discuss their future. Now saddled with a huge debt and no means to repay it, some church members wanted to declare bankruptcy. Emmy's father had a different opinion. Five days after the fire, he preached an impassioned sermon from a wagon and declared he would stay as Immanuel's pastor and assist in paying off the debt if the church council would agree to rebuild. The congregation accepted his offer and made plans to build a new church in the same location. The meeting ended with the hymn "A Mighty Fortress Is Our God," a fitting benediction.

Men, women, and children covered in black grit from charred lumber worked together to clear the debris and pile bricks to rebuild the church. Keeping his end of the bargain, Erland wrote to other churches and journeyed throughout the United States and Europe asking for money to rebuild the church. Money poured in from the East Coast and as far away as Sweden.[32]

Completed in April 1875, the church lacked a steeple, an organ, and bells; the walls remained unpainted; and there were no pews, but the congregation rejoiced just the same.[33]

That same year, Emmy and Annie finished their education at *Mamsell* Fryxell's progressive school, thought to be the finest education Sweden had to offer. Erland journeyed to Kalmar, where he had once worked as a boy, to give the commencement address.

The girls said farewell to their school chums and the threesome traveled to Älghult, Sweden, Erland's childhood home, to visit family. They stopped to see the church where their father once preached and paid their respects to family members buried in the churchyard. Erland's simple wood-framed home with its huge fireplace decorated with blue and white tiles appeared smaller to the girls than their Chicago home. After a brief stay, the trio boarded the *Polynesian* in England and set sail for America, arriving in Chicago in November 1875.[34]

While Chicago rebuilt, such was not the case for Augustana College and Theological Seminary, which faced another crisis made more severe by the depression of 1873 and subsequent financial downturn. The college needed cash and teachers. To cover the deficit, church leaders sold the print shop, including the newspaper, the *Hemlandet*. In the past eighteen years the shop had never turned a substantial profit.[35] But Emmy saw the tabloid as a spot to advertise church activities and claimed church leaders made a mistake in selling it.[36] In the years to come, both the church and the college became a source of conflict for Emmy, but for now, peace prevailed.

Chapter Two

Second Chances (1875–1883)

The devastation of the Chicago Fire and endless cleanup left Emmy's father in failing health. After preaching his last sermon at Immanuel Lutheran Church on April 5, 1875, the family said good-bye to friends, packed up their memories, and moved to Andover, Illinois. After twenty-two years, parting was bittersweet. Erland had baptized many of the church members and married still more. Others had been with him since his earliest days as a pastor, marking the end of the pioneering period.[1]

The quiet countryside of the small farming community was a striking change from the hustle and bustle of Chicago. The settlement, 175 miles west of Chicago, comprised a few crude buildings and "gumbo roads," which, in rainy weather, thickened to resemble wet concrete.

Emmy acquainted herself with country life in Andover and described these years as some of the happiest, most carefree times of her life.[2] To help with the household chores, the Carlssons hired a live-in servant, sixteen-year-old Louise Bylander. But the move failed to provide Emmy's father with any rest in body or spirit. His friend Rev. Jonas Swensson was dying. As the reverend's death drew near, he made two requests of Erland: one, that he would care for the Swensson children, for the reverend's wife was also ill, and two, that he would succeed him in the pulpit as pastor of the Andover church, one of the largest in the Augustana Synod.[3] Erland agreed to both. Emmy's parents adopted Anna Swensson, daughter of Jonas and his wife. All the while, Erland continued his responsibilities at Augustana College and Theological Seminary.

The children's orphanage was also, under the auspices of the church, adding to her father's pastoral duties. The two-story building with shutters at the windows and an arched doorway housed seventy to one hundred children[4] and needed an additional $3,000 to keep its doors open.

As her father's able assistant, Emmy helped Erland devise a plan whereby the Sunday School children would help raise the cash. She suggested mailing "Orphan Home Cards," or collection cards, to all of the Sunday schools in the Illinois conference. The children, in turn, would seek donations in support of the orphanage. Their plan worked: the children learned the importance of charity, and the moneymaking idea continued for decades throughout the Illinois conference and in other regions as well.[5]

By now, Emmy had become a beautiful eighteen-year-old with pierced ears, wire-rimmed glasses, and corkscrew curls down the nape of her neck, attracting several gentlemen callers. But she had other intentions.

Emmy took over the Andover Youth Society, which her father had organized in July 1880. She led the group with a stern hand, instilling in them a sense of responsibility. "I was told," said Emmy, "you can never get farmer boys and girls to take part. They proved to be the most punctual, reliable, alert, and active workers of any young people's society I knew. They were a happy crowd full of pep and interest. Each did their best."[6]

Aptly named the "singing young people of Andover," members of the society climbed aboard lumber wagons—large enough to carry the entire crowd—and filled the air with music as they rambled along the country roads. Anna Swensson wrote that she could hear the children singing and wondered if she were in heaven.[7] Not to be left out, Emmy and her sister, Annie, joined in the fun and fellowship dinners of chicken, turkey, and oysters.

Emmy's feminist leanings began to emerge in Andover, and she granted the girls full membership in the youth society—a first in church history.[8] Some clergy disapproved of her actions, fearing such clubs would compete with the church and cause young people to drift away from religion.[9] The confrontation gave Emmy her first taste of male dominance within the church but not her last.

With her brothers, Sam and Eben, studying at Augustana College and Theological Seminary, Emmy busied herself teaching

Swedish and the Lutheran catechism to the youngsters at church, conducting the choir, and directing the literary society in its work.[10]

An accomplished oil painter and singer, Emmy lent her talents to the orphanage school as well, teaching English, art, and music. Forty students filled the classrooms ranging in age from four to fifteen. At the close of the school year the pupils faced a thorough examination. To Emmy's credit, each passed splendidly and without error. "Miss Carlsson may be justly proud of the result of her efforts . . . not only did she enrich their minds with book learning, but their health, happiness, manners, and well living were carefully considered by her . . ." wrote a columnist for the local paper. That evening a celebration followed featuring music and drama performances, and the literary society presented a discussion titled *Shall Our Mothers Vote.*[11]

* * * *

During the mid-1880s, much of Emmy's family headed west to Lindsborg, Kansas. Nestled in the Smokey Valley region of north central Kansas, the city is still known as "little Sweden." After graduating from Augustana College, her brother Eben studied pharmacology in Chicago before moving to Lindsborg in 1884, where he wed the Carlssons' adopted daughter, Anna Swensson, on May 27, 1885. His business as a pharmacist flourished for eight years. Afterwards, he traded his drugstore for a farmer's life, while serving as the town's postmaster and dabbling in politics.[12] Eben and Anna remained in Lindsborg with their five children and Anna's aunt until their deaths.

Sam, Emmy's youngest brother, followed a different pathway until he, too, left for Kansas. Sam played an Italian Genarius violin while attending Augustana College from 1880 to 1883. While his instrument was not equal to a Stradivarius, it was considered an excellent violin. In addition, he formed an orchestral group at the college. After graduation, he settled in Lindsborg for a short time, worked as a bookkeeper, and established an orchestra in town at Bethany College.

Heeding his doctor's advice, Erland, having suffered a stroke at age sixty-seven, also moved to Lindsborg with his wife, Eva, in 1889. There they purchased a 240-acre farm complete with horses, chickens, and probably a cow or two because they had kept a milk cow while living in Chicago. Having grown up in a farming community in southern Sweden, the adventure was not an unfamiliar one for Emmy's father.[13] They called the farm Rostad, which means "place of peace." The two-story farmhouse proved to be a happy locale where friends gathered and family reunions were held. Grandchildren visited and rode the horses.[14] By all accounts, his working farm flourished.

Her brother Sam, who was once described as skillful, alert, dashing, and urbane,[15] did not stay in the quaint farming community. Seeking employment elsewhere, he returned to Chicago in the 1890s, where he took a job in the newspaper business and served as the choir director at Immanuel Lutheran Church.[16] His first wife, Tillie Edberg, passed away in 1894. He and his second wife, Pearl Curtiss, who hailed from Kansas, had two daughters, Edith and Ethel. (One source indicates Sam's wife was Pearl Lockwood, also from Kansas.)

* * * *

As her parents prepared to leave for Lindsborg, Emmy had her own aspirations. Following in her brother's footsteps, she, too, pursued a college education at Rockford Seminary for Women in Rockford, Illinois. Her friends, having gathered for a surprise going-away party, wished her well as she headed to the northern corner of Illinois.

Her dream was not unusual. Women commonly sought higher education at this time. In fact, they attended college in greater numbers than their male counterparts, and female educators outnumbered the men.[17] While female seminaries had existed since the Civil War, they were not generally academic in nature. Rockford Seminary, on the other hand, promoted scholarly pursuits and achievements, holding its students to lofty standards. (The name was shortened to Rockford College in 1892. The university became fully co-educational in 1958. Rockford College became a university in 2013.) Admission required an entrance exam, including geography and arithmetic. The curriculum prepared students for the practical duties of home and social life while instilling moral and religious principles and clear judgment. Emmy's course of study included math, science, Latin, and geography. She majored in voice, musical theory, and composition.[18]

Perched on fifteen acres along the east side of the Rock River in northern Illinois, the institution, one of several chartered schools in the state, consisted of three large brick buildings, which housed classrooms, dorm rooms, a chapel, a library, and a gym. Tuition at $275 per year included room and board. The students generally lived within a fifty-mile radius of the seminary. They came from middle-class Protestant backgrounds with stay-at-home mothers and fathers who worked as pastors, farmers, millers, or teachers.[19]

As the principal and educational legend, Anna Peck Sill stood like a pencil, thin and erect. Having grown up in the East, she fashioned the seminary after Mount Holyoke in South Hadley, Massachusetts. Deeply religious and a stern disciplinarian, Miss Peck enforced the college's strict regulations and recorded any infractions. Those who failed to comply received demerits. Emmy and the other students rose at five in the morning to do chores, such as cleaning their rooms and emptying ashes from the stove. To save on tuition, some of the girls worked at the college bussing tables and other menial tasks. Nobody could leave campus without permission. Rules forbade such vices as card playing, dancing, hair curling, and theatre. Reportedly, the food was unappealing.

To stay warm and dry, Emmy wore flannel garments, scratchy woolen hose, a waterproof cloak, and rubber overshoes, and carried an umbrella. To keep fit, everybody took one-hour walks around campus each day in their long black skirts and white shirtwaist blouses.[20] Physical exercise for women was a revolutionary idea in Emmy's day and met with some surprise.

These were pivotal times for Emmy. The students at Rockford characterized a change in social norms. The college provided them a platform from which they could break away from outdated stereotypes, test their own intellect, develop skills, and seek lasting friendships. Miss Sill, with her puritanical background, wanted to educate young women in the art of homemaking and Christian life.[21] But she, too, may have been conflicted by her own intellectual desires, feeling torn between femininity and ambition, social mores, and her own independence.

Education for the gentler sex remained controversial. Higher learning presented a conflict between self-reliance and a traditional feminine role. In the Victorian era, a woman's sphere restricted her to that of an earthly angel, who tended to every need of her family members. She was self-sacrificing, hardworking, and above all, respectable.[22] While society judged men by their abilities and intellect, it defined women by their gender, confining them to hearth and home, church, and charities. Emmy and her fellow students traversed a fine line between feminism and the conventional Victorian wisdom. The thought of Emmy competing in a male-dominated world was considered unbecoming.

To push these limits usually meant spinsterhood or vocations as missionaries, teachers, or nurses. People feared college-educated feminists would remain single and reduce the number of children born. They wondered if a woman's delicate nature could endure the strain of classroom studies.[23]

Emmy's attendance at the all-women college opened her eyes to fresh ideas, friendships, and possibilities. A good student, she graduated in 1883 after three years of study and was among the first granted a degree from the seminary. She met two extraordinary women in college who would be lifelong friends: her suitemate, Jane Addams, and Catherine Waugh (McCulloch).

Addams, who was from the small town of Cedarville, Illinois, concerned herself with reforms in public health, child welfare, and world peace. She was also an author, sociologist, suffragist, and the first American woman to receive the Nobel Peace Prize. McCulloch grew up in New Milford, Illinois. After graduating from Rockford, she pursued a law degree at Northwestern University and mobilized the charge for women's suffrage in Illinois from her home in Evanston, Illinois.

Emmy's college experiences had a pronounced influence on the rest of her life. Rockford reawakened her awareness of women's inequality with men. No longer a fanciful young girl, the suffrage movement captured her imagination. She soon began exploring intellectual endeavors outside the home and writing short magazine articles on the topic of women's rights.

* * * *

The notion of women's rights had been smoldering since the Civil War, when wives held sanitary fairs in Chicago as morale boosters. Set in a carnival-like atmosphere, the fairs featured a variety of booths, contests, and raffles. Goods donated at the fairs helped furnish hospitals, military camps, prisons, and refugees with much-needed provisions. The success of the fairs opened the doors for the women's movement in the Midwest. The idea of separate "spheres" for men and women still dominated society, however.

The Chicago Fire further ignited the suffrage movement while women focused on public welfare. But the real change came with the dawn of the Progressive movement at the close of the nineteenth century. "Progressives," born between 1850 and 1860, were the children of immigrants. Their parents, often Civil War veterans, fought the noble crusade against slavery. Like the baby boomers of the 1960s, these young people considered themselves to be a special generation.

Emmy saw the economy change from small agricultural communities to big city life. She and her peers typified the movement: middle-class city dwellers who saw themselves as social reformers, tackling major issues such as unsafe working conditions, corrupt government, poverty, tenement housing, and sweatshops. Well-educated, they admired scientific and technical discovery.

Thus, the Progressive Movement focused on social justice, history, economics, scientific methods, and more efficient ways of doing things. The women concerned themselves with party bosses, political machines, and corporate wheeler-dealers, who controlled the country's finances. They advocated prohibition and women's suffrage. When it came to social reforms, women like Emmy saw themselves as the primary agents for change.

In Chicago, the Progressive movement had its own flavor. The city was now the capital of urban sprawl—a hotbed of construction. Taller buildings called skyscrapers appeared on the city's horizon. Although the buildings were smaller than modern-day skyscrapers, they attracted young architects, such as Louis Sullivan and Daniel Burnham, to the city. State-of-the-art technology, such as the Otis elevator, which ran on electricity rather than steam, allowed movement between stories.

Housewives found chores less demanding. More servants were available, and modern conveniences, such as carpet sweepers and wringer washers, helped ease their daily chores. Mail-order catalogs from Sears and Roebuck and Montgomery Ward, both headquartered in Chicago, were a boon to shoppers everywhere.

Women had discarded their long cumbersome clothing for a more fashionable boot-length skirt. For added freedom of movement, they wore bloomers, named for Amelia Bloomer. Some scoffed that this new attire would lead to other freedoms.

Single women, who made up one-third of the Swedish immigrants settling in cities comparable to Chicago,[24] had limited job opportunities, generally working as domestics, waitresses, nurses, or midwives. At the turn of the century, the question facing many of these young female employees was, "What should the women's sphere encompass and who had the right to decide?"[25]

Emmy adhered to Christian virtues. However, her feminist viewpoints meant disregarding the biblical implication that women—created from Adam's rib—were of lesser standing. Emmy argued that differences between the sexes were a matter of nurture and not nature, a belief that would take her all the way to the US Congress as a suffragist.

Chapter Three

The Preacher's Wife (1883–1909)

As the clock ticked toward the twentieth century, Emmy began a fresh chapter in her life, one requiring her many talents. At the same time, two trends began to emerge: a huge influx of Swedish immigrants and the rapid growth of Chicago. Both would impact her future.

While the Swedes had settled in Chicago nearly forty years prior, early arrivals often trekked further west. There were now more Swedes living in the city than in Gothenburg, Sweden's second-largest city.[1] In fact, the Swedes represented 6 percent of the city's one million inhabitants, making them the third-largest ethnic group in the city behind the Germans and the Irish.[2]

Chicago's "golden era" offered modern buildings, city parks, public transportation, and most importantly, higher wages. The city with its upscale downtown was a mecca for ambitious young people and a magnet for artists and reformers, compelling immigrants to stay.

Architect Louis Sullivan built modern steel-framed skyscrapers. The "L," or elevated train, looped around the city's business district, carrying workers to their jobs and shoppers to local department stores, replacing horse-drawn carriages. Office buildings were self-contained communities with stores and restaurants, which met the needs of employees who no longer needed to leave the building.

By the late nineteenth century, a surplus of unskilled labor continued, while the economy spawned an expansion of white-collar workers—middle managers, secretaries, foremen, and salespeople, for example. Employees worked with their brain instead of brawn. Getting to work on time meant racing down the sidewalk in hopes of crossing the Chicago River before the drawbridge was lifted.[3]

The economic changes brought about a population shift outside the city's core. Streetcars extended the city's boundaries to include upscale neighborhoods, such as Hyde Park, enabling thousands of people to flow in and out of Chicago every day. The Swedes headed north to the less-congested neighborhoods of Lake View and Edgewater, which were now more accessible to the city.[4]

Change was afoot for Immanuel Lutheran Church as well. The congregation had rebuilt a church identical to the one destroyed in the Chicago Fire, and parishioners would soon call a second pastor from Sweden, Rev. Carl Anderson Evald.

Carl was born in Kil Parish, Örebro, Sweden, on May 25, 1849, to Anders Anderson and Christina Sjsquist Anderson. Located in south central Sweden, the small city of Örebro had but one major industry, shoe manufacturing. A medieval stone castle, complete with a moat, marked the city's center, exhibiting a stark contrast to America, which had not yet celebrated its centennial.

Growing up, Carl had pondered the idea of becoming a preacher and hoped someday to be a landowner. He finished his studies in the classics in 1868, graduating from Örebro University. Following his heart, he began his religious studies at age nineteen. When the Augustana Synod began recruiting young pastors to fill vacancies in newly settled areas, Carl was among the enlistees. At age twenty-two, he set sail for America on the *Tolakag* out of Liverpool, England, for a chance to fulfill his dreams. He arrived in New York City at the Castle Garden Immigration Center on August 16, 1871.[5]

Carl was a robust figure of a man in his clerical coat and preaching bands, who referred to himself as five foot nine with a high forehead, grayish-blue eyes, an Anglo-Saxon nose, and a full face. Upon reaching the shores of New York City, he may have changed his surname to Evald due to the popularity of Swedish names, such as Anderson, Carlson, and Johnson. Traditionally, it would have been "Anderson," that is, the son of Anders.

Akin with so many Swedish scholars, Carl headed for the Midwest, bound for Augustana College and Theological Seminary, which had moved from its simple beginnings in Chicago to Paxton, Illinois. Earnest in his studies, Carl completed them in 1872 at age twenty-three. After his ordination on September 29 at the Lutheran church in Galesburg, Illinois, he accepted a post in Minneapolis, which was similar in climate—cold and snowy—to his homeland. A financial crisis and controversy complicated his first year in the ministry. But he succeeded and the congregation reduced its debt, built a parsonage and a school, and eventually established a sister congregation.[6]

Carl remained in Minnesota for three years before moving on, this time to Chicago, where he was installed on April 4, 1875, as the pastor at Immanuel Lutheran Church. The congregation also dedicated the church building that day. Ample cake and coffee denoted the special occasion.

Few congregations had a closer relationship with their pastor, who acted as a spiritual guide and counselor,[7] performing baptisms with panache and grace. Friends regarded him as a model Christian gentleman and a prince among preachers. He lent his fine singing voice to the highly praised national chorus at the Auditorium Theatre in Chicago.

He had a quiet demeanor and seldom voiced his opinions at synod meetings, although he voiced his convictions when in the presence of close friends. As a modest man, Carl's silence was often more effective than his speech. Dr. John Telleen of the Augustana Synod described him this way:

> In a community of others, he [Carl] was a man of few words but spoke with thoughtful purpose. When he did speak, words flowed "like apples of gold in a pitcher of silver." His expressions—while terse in nature—were words fraught with good and laden with blessings. It was a rare treat to hear him preach, one which none would tire. He was fresh and abreast of the times.[8]

On occasion, his rich sense of humor showed through his more serious side. Dr. R. F. Weidner, a fellow pastor, spoke of him with admiration. "We met in his home beside Immanuel Lutheran Church. I became acquainted with his loveliness of character, the earnestness of his demeanor and deep interest in all church activities. I remember what joy and hilarity we spent reviewing Hebrew during my periodical visits from Rock Island, [Illinois]. It was my second home."⁹

Carl's talents in the pulpit were known within the Swedish community and the Augustana Synod. As a visitor to the Carlsson household, Carl took note of their eldest daughter. Annie, a petite twenty-year-old with porcelain features and chestnut curls which gently brushed across her shoulders, was a woman of great talent and charm. Within a year, Carl had won her heart.

Their wedding, a lovely affair, happened at Erland's church in Andover on October 4, 1876, the same year America celebrated its centennial. Glowing lanterns and colored flags marked the occasion.¹⁰ Emmy attended the wedding along with other family and friends. Folks wished the couple well and sent them on their way. The newlyweds settled in Chicago where Carl continued his pastoral duties at Immanuel Lutheran Church and Annie taught Bible classes to fifty young women.¹¹

Their happiness did not last, however. An undetermined illness struck Annie in the early years of their marriage. She and Carl departed for Sweden in June hoping to discover better medical treatment but to no avail. Annie died in Stockholm on December 27, 1880, at age twenty-four. The voyage, which had begun with such optimism, ended in a long, difficult journey home. Her casket was shipped to New York City and conveyed to Chicago, where her funeral took place. An abundance of floral arrangements surrounded her draped coffin, filling the air with sweet perfume. After the funeral, she came to rest in Graceland Cemetery in the Carlsson's family plot.

Three years passed after Annie's death, the family's grief lessened, and young hearts opened to all things possible. Emmy's relationship with her brother-in-law blossomed into love. They married in Andover on May 24, 1883, the day before his thirty-fourth birthday. Carl looked dashing in his wedding outfit. Twenty-six-year-old Emmy wore a bridal gown with appliquéd flowers and a full-length veil of tulle.

Emmy and Carl started a family immediately. Shortly before their first anniversary, they welcomed a daughter, Annie Fidelia Christina, on March 18, 1884, named in honor of Emmy's sister. A second daughter, Frances Lillian Charlotta, was born on December 2, 1886, completing the family. She was called by her middle name.

The family lived at 1662 Barry Avenue until the congregation built a parsonage at 218 Sedgwick Street, adjacent to Immanuel Lutheran Church, for the princely sum of $8,500—more than $240,000 in today's dollars.[12] The three-story brick home, Victorian in style, featured decorative moldings above the doors and windows.

The slight scent of charred wood wafted from the parlor's fireplace where several rockers and armchairs invited guests to "sit a spell." Emmy's oil paintings, one of her two daughters, and the other a country French couple, hung in the parlor. Her piano sat in an adjoining room. A formal dining room and a study, where Carl kept his books, desk, and a picture of Martin Luther, completed the first floor. The basement served as a library for young people, continuing the emphasis on Christian education that had long been a focus of the Swedes.

Carl, who parishioners considered the more reserved and studious of the two, savored quiet hours in his study, while Emmy delighted in her role as the pastor's wife, tackling her duties with energy and joy. In return, the large metropolitan congregation greatly appreciated her foresight. Some claimed Emmy could always find a solution when particularly knotty problems arose.

Houses tended to be large. Families often took in boarders and sometimes live-in servants. Census records show the Evalds shared their happy home with their fashionable teenage daughters and boarders Albestian Gassman, age thirty-three, and Albert Okerstram, a twenty-nine-year-old student from Sweden.

As a housewife, Emmy handled the most intimate details of managing a home and still had time to entertain and receive visitors at the parsonage. Immigrants coming to the city often made the Evald's home their first stop. Just as her mother had done, Emmy opened the doors of the parsonage to everyone, to the discontent of her children.

> As growing daughters in the home, my sister and I did not always relish this liberal hospitality, because much of the work fell on our shoulders. At least, we thought so. We lived in a three-story,

eighteen-room parsonage and being only a family of four, we had many rooms to spare.

Those who knew her [Emmy] only as an executive never dreamed that she also kept house. We lived in a downtown section, and curtains for the fifty-two windows, not counting the glass-paneled doors and transom, which had curtains, was a task all its own.

She painted and papered walls, supervised wash days and ironing days. Mother was a real domestic, a good cook, and a dressmaker. We girls never had a bought piece of clothing until we were eighteen years of age.

—Annie Evald Hoffsten[13]

Grandmother Eva, who lived with the family for eighteen years, also shared in the household chores.

Emmy, who never seemed to tire, had a knack for making others work just as hard. She handled many of the routine details of the church, presiding over women's groups, such as sewing circles and church socials, entertaining visitors, and shepherding future members. Her actions relieved Carl from the day-to-day church operations and allowed him more time to develop the sermons for which he was so widely famous.[14] Everybody won.

A flurry of activity occupied the household. Immanuel Lutheran Church had grown from an immigrant church to one filled with first- and second-generation worshippers. Together, the Evalds sought to meet the needs of the congregation. Emmy organized a church choir with forty-one members and created mission training programs throughout Chicago's Northwest Side. Carl called on the sick and the disadvantaged, who were of special importance to him.[15]

Prayer week, at the beginning of January, often extended for weeks with services every night. Hundreds gathered in the church basement for evening prayer meetings interspersed with song and scripture passages.[16] It appeared as though God had provided the right man for the church once again and a soul mate to help him with his tasks.

People considered the church to be a wholesome locale to meet one another. Although services continued in Swedish to maintain a connection to the old country, the church also satisfied the need to learn English. Bible classes provided the youngsters with greater exposure to the American culture and language. Three classes, held Sunday afternoons, comprised nearly four hundred students. Informal in nature, the classes allowed students to openly discuss scripture and participate in song and prayer.

Emmy, Carl, and Mary Mellander each taught a class, although Carl's pastoral duties frequently interfered with his teaching schedule, requiring a substitute. As her students could attest, Emmy preached a rousing lecture. Daughters Annie, age thirteen, and Lillian, age eleven, proved a captive audience in their mother's class. Emmy's class would become the largest of the three and outlast the other classes.[17] Emmy held the position of superintendent of the Sunday school department for twelve years. She also organized the first reunion for confirmation classes, a practice that has continued at the church for more than one hundred years.[18] Furthermore, she participated in the sewing circle and served as a deacon and hospitality secretary.

With the Evalds leading the way, Immanuel Lutheran Church grew into one of the major congregations in Chicago and the most active church in the Augustana Synod with numerous community outreach programs. But Emmy's name would become the most prominent in church history. As a pastor's wife and daughter of a well-loved pastor, she wielded a great deal of influence, despite her gender.

* * * *

During its expansion, Augustana Hospital, which Emmy's father had helped to establish, had mounting debts, and the much-needed funds were not forthcoming. Hospital executives turned to Immanuel Lutheran Church for assistance. Emmy and five other women formed a ladies' board to promote the hospital and oversee its household affairs.[19] A decade later, the Augustana women, under Emmy's direction, formed fundraising teams and challenged the men in a friendly rivalry to help raise $7,000 for the hospital. Whether the men or the women were victorious during the ten-day capital campaign is unknown. The biggest winner was the hospital, which happily sat on a pie-shaped wedge at the intersection of Garfield, Cleveland, and Lincoln Avenues.

Emmy's volunteer efforts earned her the moniker "mother of Augustana Hospital." Carl, also active in the business dealings of the hospital, served on the board for twenty-five years, the longest tenure of any board member at the time. Today, the hospital is a part of Lutheran General Hospital in Park Ridge, Illinois, where Emmy's father's portrait hangs in the hallway.

* * * *

Old beliefs remained intact, however. Restricted to home and hearth, some women depended on their housekeeping skills and abilities to achieve economic reforms in the areas of social work, nursing, and public health. As a preacher's wife, Emmy used the church to gain entrance into a man's world. She pushed others to make a difference, all the while relying on a man for guidance, that of her Lord and Savior, Jesus Christ.[20] Her persistence was evident when she accompanied Carl to the Augustana Synod conference in June 1891.

On a hillside in Chisago Lake, Minnesota, Emmy and three other clergy wives met to discuss the formation of a synod-wide woman's missionary society. They agreed to reconvene the following year at the annual conference in Lindsborg, Kansas, where Emmy's parents had resettled two years earlier.

Emmy's reputation as an organizer preceded her. "What's Emmy up to now?" asked one of the pastors.[21] Fifty women gathered at her parents' farm that June morning.

> My parents, Dr. and Mrs. Erland Carlsson, invited all the women attending the synod convention to their home on Friday afternoon, June 3, 1892. A second session was held on Saturday afternoon in Mrs. Malmberg's home, and on Monday afternoon, June 6, Alma Swensson invited us to come to her home, the Bethany

Lutheran Church parsonage. This third session was held on the beautiful lawn of the parsonage.

—Emmy Evald[22]

Pastor Swensson and his wife were longtime friends of the Carlssons dating back to their Andover, Illinois, days. But this was no ordinary *kaffeeklatsch*; as a matter of fact, some claimed that coffee was not served. Emmy, graced with her father's insight, gave a soul-stirring speech, announcing the purpose of the gathering . . . to organize a mission society comparable to what other Protestant churches had done. At first the women debated the virtues of such an organization. After long, and sometimes laughable discussions, most women approved of the idea.

They planned to form mini-missionary societies at every church throughout the synod and pattern the organization after the church with boards, committees, and auxiliaries. Representatives would preside over each territory or district. Meetings would be coordinated with the national and regional conference schedules of the synod. In addition, the woman's society wanted to manage its own resources outside of male control.[23]

But first they had to petition the men of Augustana Synod for permission to form such a group. Before presenting the idea to the synod, Mrs. Malmberg first ran the notion by a few esteemed pastors. "Excellent," said Dr. Petri. "But they [the synod] will skin you alive if you show it to them."[24] Undaunted, they marched in their long dresses and high-buttoned shoes en masse with banners waving and voices lifted, singing *"Till Verksamet"* ("Go Forward") to present their resolution. Their actions were astounding, considering women could not vote.[25]

Men shook their heads and felt free to say that such an organization bode no good. The pastors and laity debated for hours, discussing the pros and cons of such a group. Perhaps some doubted Emmy's resolve, while others failed to grasp the importance of their decision. "It is the most ridiculous and foolish thing the synod could do—give the women the right to do as they please; they do that anyway," said one pastor.[26] But Emmy was young, full of zeal for the welfare of the church, ambitious, courageous, somewhat indomitable of purpose, and the synod survived.[27] Those who initially opposed the plan yielded to the majority, the vote unanimous and the women's request granted.

The Woman's Missionary Society of the Augustana Synod was formed with the following officers: Emmy Evald, president; Alma Swensson, recording secretary; Maria Enstam, corresponding secretary; and Ida Sannquist, treasurer.[28] To handle the society's administrative duties, the Woman's Missionary Society (WMS), as it was widely known, created an executive committee and standing committees, including finance, investment, missionary education, and promotion. The organization would become one of the most exciting stories in Augustana's church history.[29]

The beginnings were humble, the membership small, and some scoffed at the idea. But despite the bumps in the road, a determined Emmy led the women onward. She clearly saw the need for such an organization and cited biblical context for it.

> [It is] the responsibility of Christian women to "Go and Tell" [the "Good News" of the Bible] and to obey the Master's commandment. . . . Vision and prayer come first, but they are not sufficient. God does not do for us what we can do for ourselves. . . .
>
> Why a woman's missionary society? Let the great organizer of world's united womanhood, Frances Willard [Organizer of the Women's Temperance Union] answer it. "Alone we can do little. Separated we are units of weakness; aggregated we become batteries of power."[30]

The women assumed that everybody wanted to take part and contribute to the society's mission. Those donating fifty cents or more automatically became members.[31] Among the first to join were Emmy's mother, her daughter Annie, and her sister-in-law.[32]

Emmy spread her message of faith and unity among women with "Go and Tell" as her motto. Filled with a strong sense of purpose, she easily persuaded others to enlist in her crusade. The membership grew, and the WMS outreach widened, winning over those who doubted whether the society could achieve its multifaceted agenda. Within a few years, more than $6,000 had been added to its coffers, and membership rose from fifty to two hundred.

The founding of the WMS began a long chapter in Emmy's life. She would serve as its president for forty-three years. No other group within the synod was so well organized and well-managed as the WMS.

* * * *

Chicago buzzed with talk of a world's fair far greater than the one held in Paris in 1889. The Columbian Exposition was intended to commemorate the four hundredth anniversary of Christopher Columbus's discovery of America in 1492; however, due to the country's financial recession, the festivities were scheduled for 1893.

St. Louis, New York City, and Washington, DC, all wished to hold the event. But Chicago's central location made it a logical choice—at least for those who lived there. The city had overcome cholera, a devastating fire, and riots in Haymarket Square. Still, some outsiders thought Chicago to be a vulgar, uneducated, and uncouth area. The US Congress made its final selection in 1890, choosing Chicago to host the fair, which meant the city had just three years to complete its plans. Officials decided upon the southern side of the city, which is now Jackson Park, as the perfect location.

Daniel Burnham, the father of city planning for Chicago, was well known for raising the streets of Central Chicago to make way for sewers and better sanitation. Up until then, Lake Michigan was contaminated, and the downtown area was an unsightly mess, totally taken over by railway cars and warehouses. But his greatest achievement so far would be the Columbian Exposition. Easily one of the greatest public relations coups in Western history, it would become the gold standard for future world's fairs.

Although the fair's classical architecture reflected that of ancient Rome, Paris, and other grand cities of Europe, its design represented the future of the Chicago. A variety of colors might have been used, but in the interest of time, the planning committee decided every building should be painted a gleaming white.

Emmy clipped several articles about the fair and women's roles from of *The Daily Inter Ocean* newspaper, but whether she went to the expo is uncertain. Given the fair's popularity, the Evalds probably were among the estimated twenty-seven million visitors. They may have watched as President Cleveland opened the fair with a flourish as he pushed the button powering all the machinery. Flags waved majestically, and a flock of snow-white doves soared in the air.[33]

The Columbian Exposition was open for only six months from May 1, 1893, to October 30, 1893. The fairgrounds were surrounded by water, allowing visitors to enter the buildings by land or boat for a Venetian flair. The Evalds could have strolled the Midway Plaisance or carnival area, which stretched more than seven hundred acres. They may have sipped water from drinking fountains, a technological advancement, or listened to John Philip Sousa play a march at the dedication of the fair.

Emmy might have dared to ride Mr. Ferris's creation, a giant steel wheel, which took riders higher in the air than they had ever been. A twenty-five-minute ride cost fifty cents. The family could have heard yodelers from Germany, ridden on a camel, or marveled at Buffalo Bill and Annie Oakley with guns blazing along the Midway. Her daughters might have sampled treats, such as Cracker Jack, Juicy Fruit gum, and Shredded Wheat, although the latter was not a huge success with visitors.

A columnist for the *The Daily Inter Ocean* newspaper noted the abundance of pretty girls at the fair, claiming that they were the "best exhibit of all," further citing that businessmen were at work during the week. Vice President Adlai Stevenson comments on the fair related to the weather, ". . . you Chicagoans do things in such a rush that you pass in one day from winter to summer and never give spring a chance."[34] Weary of the locals' boasting of the fair's triumphs, a *New York Sun* reporter allegedly referred to Chicago as the "Windy City."

Thirty-eight states and territories had exhibits at the fair, with Illinois being the largest state building. Most visitors headed to the state pavilion first before taking in the rest of the sights.

Nearly twenty countries were also represented. Emmy would have beamed with pride at the Swedish Pavilion, which included artwork by Anders Zorn and exhibits of manufacturing and mining, illustrating Swedish technology. Each nation had a special day for celebrating its heritage. July 20 was designated Swedish Day. A large downtown parade kicked off the event in the morning with bystanders lined up along the sidewalk waving to friends. More than 650 people, and possibly the Evalds, attended an afternoon concert in the park and fireworks that evening, a tribute to the Swedes' influence on the city of Chicago.[35]

* * * *

The expo provided a platform for women's rights, illustrating their diversity and showcasing their talents outside of the home, as well as living conditions for the gentler sex, who became the target of domestic abuse.

As word of the world's fair spread, activist and suffragist Susan B. Anthony saw an opportunity to promote her agenda. She launched a campaign for the inclusion of women on the fair's governing board. In time, the men approved her request and created a "Board of Lady Managers" as an honorary appointment. However, as a token concession, no one expected the women to actively participate.[36]

Bertha Palmer, wife of Potter Palmer and grand dame of Chicago, was elected president of the Lady Managers and used her wealth and influence to ensure the woman's point of view was heard. She did not endorse woman's suffrage. However, she did open her house, a stately mansion on the shore of Lake Michigan, for meetings and receptions to aid a variety of causes. She determined a woman could be more influential if she were apolitical and—indeed—she was proof of that. Her wealth and position as Mrs. Potter Palmer yielded her tremendous power among the rich and famous.

Largely the result of the Lady Managers, the Women's Building became a reality—the first of its kind to be built by a female architect. Sophia Hayden, a graduate of the Massachusetts Institute of Technology, designed the building, which backed up to the Midway. The area is now the front yard of the University of Chicago.

The building included a day-care center and dormitory for women who could not afford pricey hotels. More importantly, it gave women an opportunity to work beside men, express their ideas, and prove that they could accomplish great things. Because social issues, such as day care, were being entrusted to the fairer sex, their influence widened.[37]

Although the women gained power and budgetary control over the Women's Building, much to their chagrin, not even Emmy had enough influence to close the shocking display of gyrating belly dancing. Several exotic dancers performed at the expo. The most popular one was "Little Egypt," which was the stage name commonly associated with Fatima Djemille.

* * * *

The Columbian Exposition was a secular event. The year before it opened, a Presbyterian pastor, Rev. John Barrows, proposed a religious world's fair to show what God had wrought. He believed mutual lessons might be learned by mingling the fundamental beliefs of world regions. The novel idea was historic. The congress opened on September 11, 1893, and allowed for formal discussions among people of all religions.

> There is nothing in history which stands as a precedent for the great congresses which are to be held during the period of the World's Columbian Exposition. It was deemed eminently fitting that amid so much that was to show to the world the material progress of man that some exposition should be made of what has been achieved in the past in the realms of intellectuality.
>
> —*The Sunday Inter Ocean*[38]

The congress ran concurrently with the world's fair on the fairgrounds. Those who attended were certain the memory of the World Congress of Religions, now known as the Parliament of the World's Religions, would long outlast that of the dazzling "White City."[39]

The gathering of different faiths represented most of the world's population. Its purpose was to achieve peace and a tolerance among all religions. People from around the world—Catholics and

Confucians, Methodists and Muslims—came together. The Shinto priests in their flowing robes, Buddhist monks in garments of white and yellow, and the Greek Orthodox archbishop attired in a black veil and royal purple robe were all present.[40]

There was some concern, however. Many of the participating groups had previously met on the battlefield. Would they come in peace? Because an overwhelming number of attendees were of different faiths, some feared a possible backlash against Christianity.[41] What role would women play? There was no immediate answer.

Because the women were thought to be too timid and uneducated, they were not originally part of the planning process. But with the acceptance of the board of lady managers, a World Congress Auxiliary was established, with Bertha Palmer presiding along with Ellen Henrotin, activist and suffragist. This huge undertaking included more than five hundred women from twenty-seven countries serving on the advisory council.[42]

The groups met at the north end of the park in Washington Hall at the Art Palace. May Wright Sewell served as chair for the International Council of Women. A total of eighty-one meetings were conducted, some of which ran concurrently. The crowds grew to more than a hundred and fifty thousand, with more than three hundred speeches.[43] Representatives from all walks of life attended the congress, including several distinguished women such as Frances Willard; Mary Baker Eddy, founder of the Christian Science Church; and Julia Ward Howe, social activist and author of the "Battle Hymn of the Republic."

Lydia H. Dickinson opened the general session with an address on the "Cooperation of Men and Women," crystallizing the women's viewpoints on suffrage:

> Women's suffrage does not mean, as has been charged, a desire on the part of women to be like men or to assume essential masculine duties and prerogatives. God takes care of that. In most it is the desire of an acorn to become an oak and nothing else. Thus, a woman's need for self-fulfillment does not negate her role as wife and mother but allows her to meet her destiny.[44]

Dickinson's presentation set the tone for the meetings that followed. Well-known suffragists such as Lucy Stone, Jane Addams, Elizabeth Cady Stanton, and Susan B. Anthony preached on equality, reform, and solidarity among women. Attendees also heard speeches on humanity and religious tolerance, marriage, education, science, and philosophy. Other sessions included presentations on different faiths. In addition to the general meetings, each religious denomination held its own caucus.[45]

Emmy organized the Woman's Lutheran Congress as chairman along with eighteen others in the home of May Mellander and received a medal for her contribution to the congress. "The door of opportunity was opened when the committee from the Columbus World's Fair in Chicago appointed me president of the 'First World's Congress of Lutheran Women in the World' in 1891. What a privilege to meet the leading and consecrated women of the world," said Emmy.[46]

Due to her father's illness, Emmy did not attend the meetings as scheduled. Instead, a committee member, Mellander, led discussions with Lutheran women from around the world, including Denmark, Finland, Germany, Norway, Iceland, India, and Sweden, and six Lutheran church organizations within the United States.[47] Participants paid their own travel expenses and stayed with Lutheran families in the area.

The Lutheran Congress meetings, conducted on the evenings of September 14 and 15, 1893, revolved around women's roles within the church and allowed for an exchange of ideas. Although several speeches were steeped in conservative thinking, thus reflecting the current views of the Lutheran church, the intent was to better understand the position, duties, and power of Lutheran women around the world.

On the opening day of the Lutheran Congress, Palmer and Henrotin gave the welcoming addresses. Numerous speeches were given, and papers presented with a focus on women in the church. Nellie Blessing Eyster's speech on "Women's Influence upon Church and Home" enumerated ways in which mothers can influence their families and keep them on a "straight-and-narrow" path.

The second day opened with a discussion of synod history. Emma B. Scholl of Baltimore proposed that women's well-developed instincts made them excellent Sunday school teachers able to recognize the children's needs and produce the desired outcomes. The afternoon sessions focused on the work of deaconesses and their personal sacrifices as ministers to the impoverished. The final speaker was Dr. A. S. Kugler from India, who recounted her experiences in the mission fields over the previous twelve years and the harsh realities for Hindu women, who were in dire need of a hospital.[48] (Emmy eventually collected the necessary means to build a hospital in Rajahmundry, India.)

The World Congress of Religions concluded with Handel's "Hallelujah Chorus" on September 17, 1893. Because the congress provided a forum for the exchange of ideas on an intellectual, spiritual, and artistic level, it was considered the most significant assembly of women ever held, calling for equal opportunities, educational privileges, professional activity, and equal wages for equal work.[49] Rather than an ending, a tradition began. Religious leaders have continued to gather in different countries for more than one hundred years for the congress.

After all the hoopla, the Chicago Exposition closed with a whimper in October 1893. A large grand finale had been planned. But when a disgruntled employee assassinated Mayor Carter Henry Harrison outside of his home, the event was canceled to allow the city to mourn. Unsure of what to do with the buildings, the city let most of them collapse and decay. Only two buildings survived: the Fine Arts Building, which became the nucleus of Chicago's Museum of Science and Industry, and the Art Institute's first permanent building. The Ferris wheel was torn down and rebuilt for the St. Louis World's Fair in 1904. On July 5, 1894, less than a year since its closing, vandals burned what remained of the White City.[50] When it ended, the fair and not the World Congress of Religions etched its mark on the city.

While the buildings may have crumbled, the strides women had made showed them to be capable and creative. Women would continue to work toward greater equality into the next millennium.

Shortly before the close of the fair, Emmy's father had another stroke while visiting relatives in the Scandinavian community of Sister Bay in Door County, Wisconsin. Having preached what would be his final sermon, Erland returned to Chicago with Eva and lived with the Evalds until Erland's death on October 19, 1893, at the age of seventy-one.

The funeral began at two in the afternoon at Immanuel Lutheran Church. Friends from Augustana College and Theological Seminary and Bethany College attended as well as others who came from across the country to pay their respects. A church quartet sang one of Erland's favorite hymns, "Rock of Ages."

The service ran long due to the numerous telegrams and eulogies. The funeral procession, more than one mile in length, did not reach Graceland Cemetery until nightfall. The sexton lit a lantern so the graveside service could continue. The effect was deeply moving as its amber glow cast a dim shadow over the open grave. Twenty-five hundred mourners attended the ceremony.[51]

* * * *

The leaders of the Woman's Lutheran Congress remained in contact after the fair closed and formed the Lutheran Woman's League of Chicago and Vicinity on October 19, 1894. Emmy presided as president for six years.[52] The association sponsored two charitable causes of note: first, the "Relief Day" activities at Immanuel Lutheran Church, which assisted victims of the San Francisco earthquake with clothing and bedding; and second, the founding of the Maywood Receiving Home in Maywood, Illinois, to care for orphaned and neglected children.[53] In addition to the Maywood home, Emmy helped establish a second orphanage, the Orphan's Home Society in Joliet, Illinois, and served as its president, recalling her early days at the Andover, Illinois, orphanage.

Major changes lay ahead for Emmy and Immanuel Lutheran Church as the "Gilded Age," as Mark Twain described it, came to an end. The importance of Swede Town had diminished, and church membership, which had peaked in 1887, soon followed. Whereas Sunday school attendance had steadily increased up until

1903, after that, fewer young people came to church, and attendance dropped by nearly 90 percent. The cause was threefold. The "L" made it possible for folks to commute into the city from nearby neighborhoods, which were less noisy and more affordable. Areas ten miles outside the city, known as suburbia, were conveniently located near train stations. As church members ventured farther out of the city, their children attended Sunday schools closer to home. In addition, the times were more prosperous, and Poles, Hungarians, and Russians, to name a few, were moving into the downtown area, altering the city's ethnic composition. Finally, with greater industrialization in Sweden, immigration to America also began to slow and came to a virtual halt by World War I.

As Immanuel Lutheran Church celebrated its fiftieth anniversary, Carl kept a watchful eye on the shifting demographics and proposed the idea of building a church in a different section of the city where many members now resided.[54] Eventually, the congregation did move outside the city center to the Edgewater area. But for the time being, Emmy and Carl busied themselves organizing the Golden Jubilee celebration at Immanuel Lutheran Church, which occurred on January 16–18, 1903. Hundreds of people arrived in Chicago to participate in the festivities. Various luminaries gave speeches, and five hundred people attended the evening banquet.[55] In recognition of this milestone, the church published its first memorial book, largely the work of Emmy. The *Minnes-Skrift* documented the church's illustrious history with facts and photos.[56]

More excitement followed when the Evalds' eldest daughter, Annie, announced her engagement to Rev. Conrad Hoffsten, an Augustana graduate. The young couple married in May 1904. The bride's wedding dress was a confection of lace, while the groom dressed in a tuxedo. More than a dozen bridesmaids participated in the wedding, each wearing a long white dress trimmed with rows of lace and a high collar. Every attendant carried a bouquet of long-stemmed red roses. The reverend and his bride served Salem Lutheran Church, an outgrowth of Immanuel Lutheran Church, on Chicago's South Side.

* * * *

Emmy and Carl eagerly supported faith-based projects within the community despite its changing population. In April 1907, the Evalds and twenty-three church members formed the Immanuel Woman's Home Association.[57] Although it was not a legal entity of the church, the association planned to establish a Christian home where young working women—most of whom were immigrants—could live in a safe, comfortable environment. Their initiative, purely philanthropic, did not turn a huge profit.[58] They recognized the many dangers found in a big city and feared young, friendless women might fall prey to temptation. As a big believer in the project, Carl served as the first president of the association. Emmy presided as vice president and then as president from 1909 to 1935.[59] For Emmy, the venture was the first of many such homes for women.

The first building, purchased in July 1907 for $7,500, featured multiple stories and a stone façade. Three association members donated the money for a down payment. The location at 1505 North LaSalle Street proved idyllic, given its proximity to downtown, the Lincoln Park Zoo, and Immanuel Lutheran Church. The doors opened on August 7, making the association's dreams a reality. The home, which had a large office area and a grand reception parlor, housed twenty women. The residents came from every state in the nation and twenty different nationalities, most of whom were Scandinavian. Rooms filled quickly. In the first year, more than two hundred women passed through its entryway.

The women worked in a variety of professions, including office work, dressmaking, nursing, and educational endeavors. Rates reflected the small salaries that the women earned. Guests paid up to four dollars per week for rent, except in the case of illness.[60] Residents participated in devotions and Bible studies on a regular basis. Social activities, including birthday and holiday parties, and other special occasions, led to long-term friendships among the women.

As word spread, the association purchased four more buildings to meet the demand. Three of the buildings were on North Street next to the original home, and a fifth building faced the rear lot. All total, the homes provided room for 165 female guests.[61]

Cash donations helped cover expenses, and linen "showers" provided household goods. Because two hundred sheets, four hundred towels, and one hundred or more pillowcases were normally sent out to a local laundry, improvements, such as a home laundry equipped with a washing machine, dryer, and mangle, saved money. The residents could also do their personal laundry.[62]

Supporters stood on street corners with collection cans asking passersby for donations during citywide "Tag Day" events. In return, contributors received a tag to show they had donated, a tradition that charities continue to use in the streets of Chicago. Emmy, dubbed a "miracle of energy," worked to obtain donations of food and materials for the homes.

During the Great Depression, men also came to the home, waiting patiently outside the La Salle buildings for any type of handout. When the task of feeding them became overwhelming, they were referred to city-sponsored options.[63] (The Immanuel homes provided young women room and board for fifty years before erecting an apartment complex in 1957 at Clark and LaSalle Streets.)

By now Emmy presided over five different organizations, including the WMS, Augustana Hospital, and the church. Countless meetings, planning, and assorted tasks may have overwhelmed most, but not Emmy, whose business savvy and organizational skills enabled her to meet the demands of a hectic schedule.

* * * *

Emmy and Carl celebrated their twenty-fifth wedding anniversary at a surprise party given for them by the church in May 1908.[64] The couple had shared much happiness over the years, but it would soon come to an end. Carl fell gravely ill the following year, experiencing great pain. As death neared, Emmy kept his room dimly lit and the drapes drawn to invoke a spirit of calm. His mind slipping as his kidneys began to fail, he called to Emmy as she entered the room, but the name he used was "Annie," Emmy's sister's, his first wife.

Carl died from Bright's disease on March 13, 1909, just shy of his sixtieth birthday. He had served Immanuel Lutheran Church as its pastor for thirty-four years. No other Swedish pastor had delivered more sermons to so many people. During those years, his message had been heard by all classes of people. In his eulogy, Dr. Telleen, a longtime friend, had this to say: "Carl Evald was one of the most complete, full and rounded-out characters it has been my pleasure to know. To his congregation, he was a shepherd, caring for all, calling on homes and welcoming people to his house at all hours."[65]

The finality of his passing deeply saddened the congregation. A hushed quiet filled the sanctuary where his body laid in state. Muffled whispers and the clicking of heels could be heard as lines of mourners shuffled past his black casket. Salty tears glistened on their cheeks. Some bowed their heads and others reached to touch the casket as they paid their respects.

Entrance to the funeral service required a ticket. Mourners filled three large balconies. Strains of the opening hymn, "Nearer My God to Thee," could be heard by those standing outside in the soft rain. Crowds spilled into the streets, blocking traffic, as they waited to say farewell to their pastor. Six funeral carriages laden with flowers made their way to Graceland Cemetery, where Carl came to rest near his father-in-law.[66] He would be remembered as one of the outstanding orators in the Augustana Synod, and above all, a man of God. (In October 1911, Carl Evald's remains were reinterred in the family plot that Emmy had purchased at Graceland Cemetery.)

After Carl's death, Emmy moved her membership from Immanuel Lutheran Church to Salem Lutheran Church in Chicago where her son-in-law Dr. Hoffsten preached in English and Swedish. She then affiliated with the Bethel Church in Chicago, which eventually merged with Immanuel Lutheran Church, making her once again a member of her childhood church.[67]

In May 1909, at age 52, Emmy bought two apartments on Winthrop Avenue within an easy stroll of Lake Michigan for $14,000.[68] One apartment housed her mother and the other herself and her daughter Lillian. On occasion, her grandchildren delighted in sleepovers on Emmy's convertible sofa in the living room. Before bed, they bent down at her knee to say their prayers.[69]

Twenty-three-year-old Lillian attended the Columbia College of Expression at 616 South Michigan Avenue. A pretty woman who loved poetry, Lillian, like her mother, exhibited artistic abilities through her needlework and china painting. She had been especially fond of her father who, she claimed, never raised his voice, and she regretted he would not be there to walk her down the aisle when it came time for her to marry. She may also have been her father's favorite because her sister, Annie, seemed more businesslike.

In time, Lillian, too, found love. She met Amel Carlson on a hayride at Immanuel Lutheran Church. He sealed their fate with a moonlight kiss among the earthy bales of golden hay. Amel stood five foot ten with a strong jawline, wavy brown hair, and dark eyes to match. Originally from Stephenson, Michigan, he, too, came from Swedish stock. After graduating from Augustana College, Amel took a job in Chicago as a general clerk with a streetcar company.

The couple wed on October 25, 1911. The bride, with light brown hair and sparkling blue eyes, wore a simple gown with an empire waist. Amel wore a waistcoat and bow tie. Emmy's joy mixed with sadness. Both of her daughters had married Augustana graduates with promising futures and lived nearby. Her mother, Eva, had died of pneumonia in July of that year. As a widow, she was now alone—her parents passed away and her children grown.

Chapter Four

Getting the Vote (1895–1920)

Nine years before Emmy's birth, Stanton, Stone, and others met in Seneca Falls, New York, in 1848. Radical in their thinking, these early suffragists claimed women were equal to men as they crisscrossed the country in hopes of gaining grassroots support and encouraging others to organize. Of course, not everyone agreed. Some women thought their husbands should vote for them. Others argued that women lacked the emotional makeup necessary to vote. Still others presumed women had all the rights they needed. Could suffrage mean lower wages for men supporting families? Were women so overburdened with household chores that they lacked time to learn the issues? Would suffrage lead to an increase in divorce? Who would speak for the widows and the unmarried? Any number of questions were raised by women on both sides of the suffrage issue.

Few men supported a woman's right to vote, claiming that what a man admires in a woman is called femininity. Take a woman who wears bloomers and uses modern methods, and she is different from what nature intended.[1]

Sentiments such as these doused ice water on the suffrage quest, but the women carried on in the belief that the vote enabled them to cast an opinion to which they were entitled. They argued that men, too, needed women's suffrage to provide more backbone in the legislative halls.[2]

By the mid-1850s, women formed small groups or societies to aid the Civil War effort. They held sanitation fairs and fundraisers to purchase medical necessities. Many looked after the family farm and conducted day-to-day business activities. By the 1860s, women made up nearly 50 percent of the Illinois population.

Emmy's mother listed her occupation as "housekeeper" in the census records, which was typical of most women who managed the home, served as hostess, and performed other wifely duties. Only a few states allowed married women to control their own earnings or obtain custody of their children in the case of a divorce.

With the coming of the industrial age and greater urbanization, old ideas began to dissolve, allowing the women's movement to gain steam. A cultural revolution began to emerge like a butterfly from its cocoon. Industrial expansion meant a change in women's roles, such as more employment opportunities outside the norm in the fields of medicine and law. An increase of career choices led to greater financial independence. They began gathering and asserting themselves politically, calling for social reforms in the areas of education and temperance. They formed alliances and channeled their efforts toward the public good.

Nonetheless, the fight for women's suffrage would be a long uphill battle—one Emmy would eventually join, marching arm in arm with Anthony and other well-known suffragists. Of course, many women were involved in the movement on the national level and in Illinois. Presented here are those women who were known to be acquainted with Emmy.

When a bill passed the Illinois legislature allowing married women to keep their own wages, the suffragists buzzed with excitement. Their optimism faded with the passage of the Fourteenth Amendment in 1868 that specified "males" as voters. The ratification of the Fifteenth Amendment granted suffrage to males regardless of race, color, or previous servitude but failed to extend this right to women, bringing more disappointment.

Bent but not bowed, the suffragists continued their crusade during Emmy's formative years. Two organizations were formed in 1869 that took center stage in the fight for women's rights during the nineteenth century: The National Woman Suffrage Association (NWSA) and the American Woman Suffrage Association (AWSA). The latter focused more on a state-by-state effort.

That same year, Anthony and Stanton came to Chicago to promote women's rights. Their actions gave birth to the Illinois Woman Suffrage Association (IWSA). As president, Mary Livermore organized the first convention. The public response smacked of sexism. A *Chicago Tribune* reporter wrote that women lacked the ability to govern, let alone organize a convention.[3] Courageously, they pushed forward.

Some recall the weather being particularly temperate. By 1888, winter temperatures in Chicago stayed above zero until March—a historical record for the Windy City—and record heat plagued the city the following summer. As temperatures warmed up, the suffrage movement came alive.

The next generation of suffragists now led the campaign. They tended to be well educated and married to professional men, such as preachers, lawyers, publishers, and editors. Among them were two of Emmy's college classmates: McCulloch and Addams. Willard, dean of women at Northwestern University, participated in the movement along with several other notable Illinois women. Strategic in their efforts, they learned how to network. Emmy's home state emerged as a dominant force in the movement and a model for other states.

Women experienced more freedoms in dress and transportation as well. The dress code changed from the full-busted woman to a newly defined female beauty—the "Gibson Girl." Named for Charles Dana Gibson's illustrations in *Collier's* magazine, dresses worn by the Gibson Girl emphasized a more natural hourglass figure with a full skirt and narrow waist. The fit suited the women who competed alongside their male counterparts in athletics and participated in physical fitness, including riding the ever-popular bicycle. Tea dresses or lingerie dresses were also popular for afternoon attire. Beautiful slips showed through the open cutwork. The lack of a corset provided greater comfort.

This modern freedom raised a few eyebrows, however. Some suggested women would be able to travel to meet their boyfriends without benefit of a chaperone, a scandalous suggestion. Evanston's own Willard rode her bike, named Gladys, and symbolically equated her conquest of the two-wheeler with the need for women to assert themselves within a male-dominated society.

My first appearance in politics occurred when Catherine Waugh, as she was then, and Jane Addams and I went to the Illinois State House in Springfield to lobby for a bill which we had drawn urging the age of consent or girls be raised to sixteen instead of fourteen as it was then.

The men were incredulous that women concerned themselves with this question, which they believed to be strictly men's business.

—Emmy Evald

Emmy scolded them with the warning that once women had the vote, they would change the law. The men retorted that they would wait until then.[4]

In 1891, cheers went up when the women of Illinois could vote in school board elections. Although many officials were appointed rather than elected, the door to the vote opened slightly. Resembling that of a steam train rushing for the coast, the movement picked up speed as women rushed to take advantage of the legislation.

Emmy's generation, the Progressives, had graduated from afternoon socials to addressing the more serious issues of prohibition, sanitation, child labor laws, and pure food. They fought to eliminate laws based on gender that prevented them from voting, holding office, and serving on a jury. The women assembled at state conventions to discuss issues such as education, divorce, property rights, and equal pay. To keep the momentum going, McCulloch changed the name of the IWSA to the Illinois Equal Suffrage Association (IESA). Annual dues were one dollar, or a lifetime membership cost ten dollars. Subscriptions to the *Illinois Suffragist* cost twenty-five cents per year.

As the struggle for suffrage intensified, working women of different ethnic and middle-class backgrounds united. In Chicago, women made progress toward municipal enfranchisement. Although they lacked a win, the taste of victory inched one step closer. From 1893 until 1913, suffragists sent bills to every session of the Illinois legislature.

At age thirty-eight, Emmy's zest for life remained strong, all while raising her family, leading the WMS, and continuing her volunteer work. In 1895, she led a group of women to Springfield, Illinois, where she addressed the Illinois state legislature on behalf of women's suffrage. The delegates hoped to secure the passage of the township suffrage bill but were once again defeated.

Emmy considered herself a Republican—the party of Presidents Abraham Lincoln and Teddy Roosevelt. Her husband, Carl, also a Republican, championed women's rights as well. Decades later, Emmy, who described herself as timid, wrote to McCulloch, "I laugh now how much you had to urge me to speak to the Illinois senators and representatives at Springfield. It gave me courage to see many of my Sunday school boys there and my fright was gone."[5]

With her fears allayed, Emmy forged ahead with members of the IESA, presenting bills before the Illinois legislators that would allow women to vote in presidential elections and for county and city officials. In December 1897, the IESA put forth a bill exempting women who owned property from taxation, claiming it amounted to taxation without representation. The bill, which caught the interest of the press and the people of Illinois but not the legislators, failed.

* * * *

Women's organizations formed along ethnic and religious lines, moving their agendas forward. They hoped for more autonomy outside the realm of home and church, thereby transforming their experiences in the home for the greater good. Emmy's work with Augustana Hospital exemplified how women used the church structure to benefit public health, nursing, and social work.

Inspired by her friend Carrie Chapman Catt, who addressed the Illinois suffrage convention, Emmy founded an organization of her own and served as its president. The Swedish-American Woman's Equality Association of Chicago, with its seventy-five members, remained the only one of its kind, even though there were more than two million Swedes living in the country.

By banding together in support of women's rights, Emmy hoped to expose Swedish American women to spiritual and intellectual opportunities, as well as social and political pursuits. Emmy, who was once described as "a bright-eyed, energetic-looking, little woman who is intently interested in woman's suffrage,"[6] conducted active letter-writing campaigns to attract noteworthy speakers who would further the cause of women's suffrage.

Club members held monthly meetings in their homes because male relatives did not approve of public gatherings.[7] Women generally wished to avoid the limelight. But one assembly caught the eye of a reporter for the Sunday edition of the *Chicago Daily Tribune*.[8]

The group rallied in Phoenix Hall at East Division Street in Chicago. The program, which included nineteen speakers, began at eight in the evening with the singing of "America," after which Emmy Evald greeted the crowd. In her remarks, she pointed out that Sweden stood out as the first country to grant women [conditional] equal suffrage.

> Since 1869, the women of Sweden have voted for every office their husbands, sons, fathers, or brothers have voted for and we Swedish women who have become Swedish Americans are asking the Lord to give us an understanding to do our duty in this country—to awaken a deeper and stronger love for the country in which we live.
>
> Anything that makes a woman freer develops her moral, intellectual, and spiritual life makes her a true mother and a queen of her home.
>
> —Emmy Evald[9]

Proud of her heritage, Emmy often espoused women's rights in Sweden in hopes of gaining the same liberties for women in America. Several prominent people attended the rally, including McCulloch, two judiciary officials, and two Illinois state senators. Judge Murray Tuley called inequality "a crime that keeps one-half of the people from exercising the right of self-government."[10] Other speakers talked about temperance. They surmised the consumption of alcohol to be the downfall of the American family and one of the leading causes of sunstroke, infant mortality, and traffic accidents. Eight hundred women attended the meeting, which lasted until midnight.[11]

As interest in public affairs grew, women began forming clubs, which provided them an intellectual stimulus but did not detract from their more domesticated roles as wives and mothers. Typically from the well-to-do middle class, they affiliated with clubs to gather support for their cause and build coalitions. The women's goals focused on social activism, especially as it related to women and children. They championed the arts as well.

In 1900, the Chicago club season opened with a wide agenda, including human interest topics and home improvements. The *Chicago Daily Tribune* reported that "the clubs would lift up the women's status in the first years of the twentieth century, advancing an organized society."[12]

Recognizing that the Chicago Woman's Club would aid her in her work and stimulate her intellectually, Emmy petitioned her friends and acquaintances, including Addams, Henrotin, and McCulloch, to sponsor her membership. The club with its five hundred members provided a foray into the business world. While women could easily survive within the political arena, without a voice in the government, they were powerless to effect the changes they envisioned for Chicago. So Emmy and her friends sought alternative methods to accomplish their plans.

McCulloch and Addams led the charge to Springfield, Illinois, with Addams lecturing from the back of the train platform along the way, but a win in the state legislature continued to elude them. Illinois represented a man's world. A married woman's duties revolved around childcare and maintaining a Christian household. However, as the size of the suffrage movement broadened, more women began to recognize its necessity. Aggressive campaigns were carried out with great enthusiasm. Suffrage leaders now garnered greater respect among their sisters, and the women kept on marching to the state capital.

As a forceful speaker, Emmy was called upon to address different groups. She learned the hard way that arrangements were not always made beforehand, causing her to scurry about to locate meeting rooms and other accommodations. Citing that her time was too valuable and precious to tend to such matters, she declined last-minute invitations.

* * * *

The NWSA and the AWSA merged in 1890, creating the National American Woman Suffrage Association (NAWSA). Acquaintances and close friends regarded Emmy, a charter member of the organization and an active participant, as a doer and social activist. As Petrus Olaf Bersell, president of Augustana Synod, tells it: "In raising the women to an unprecedented level of activity and authority and joining in the national movement of greater political participation of women, Emmy Evald proved to be a forerunner of the 'liberation movement' of more recent times."[13] Passionate in her beliefs, Emmy became more involved on a national level.

Fifty years after the first women's rights convention in New York, NAWSA scheduled the thirtieth women's convention in Washington, DC. Leaving two teenage daughters and a husband behind, Emmy headed to the nation's capital. Carl, a supportive spouse, remained in Chicago, balancing his church responsibilities with housekeeping duties.

The convention was held February on 13–19, 1898, at the Columbia Theatre on Twelfth and F Streets. Seating for the day sessions was free. A free-will offering was the price of admission for the evening sessions. Reserved seats cost twenty-five cents.

The agenda consisted of business and committee meetings and speeches that were presented early in the week. On Thursday evening, February 17, Rev. Frederic Hinckley of Philadelphia read a paper on "The Civil Rights of Women," and McCulloch closed the evening session with an address on "The Economic Status of Women."

Emmy took the podium Friday evening. Her speech on "The Work of Swedish Women in America" clearly illustrated the advantages that Swedish women enjoyed and took the audience by storm.

When Emmy declared that women have lived in the United States since 1638 and have yet to vote, her statement created a stirring discussion, during which a woman jumped up and yelled, "I come from Wilmington, Delaware, and I know Mrs. Evald speaks the truth." The woman's response brought a hardy laugh.[14]

Other notable speakers participated in the convention. Alice Stone Blackwell, a prominent WCTU activist and editor of the

Woman's Journal, gave a presentation along with Rev. Anna Shaw, the first female to be ordained by the Methodist Church. Emmy's friend Catt participated as well. The convention closed with a tribute to WCTU organizer Willard. Final remarks were given by NAWSA President Anthony.[15] Women were asked to bring their train tickets to the final meeting as transit information would be available.

Four years later Emmy received an invitation to serve as a delegate to the International Woman's Suffrage Conference in Washington, DC, where the fight for equal rights persisted at the thirty-fourth annual NAWSA convention on February 12–18, 1902.

She had hoped her brother Sam could purchase her ticket to defray her traveling expenses. Such was not the case, and she wrote to the Johnsons, friends in New York, whose generosity had paid her expenses once before, and who agreed to do so again.

The First Presbyterian Church, built in 1827, housed the delegates. Located between C and D Streets (formerly named John Marshall Plaza), the church had been attended by several US presidents, including Andrew Jackson, James Polk, Franklin Pierce, and Grover Cleveland. (The city razed the building in the 1930s.) The pastor at the time, Rev. T. Dewitt Talmage, embraced liberal viewpoints. Conversely, his predecessor, Rev. Byron Sutherland, had argued against the suffrage movement more than once.[16]

More than one thousand women filled the pews and spilled into the parlor rooms. An array of flowers decorated the platform. Clara Barton, founder of the American Red Cross, had graciously provided thirty national flags from different countries for the convention in hues of vibrant reds, cornflower blues, crisp greens, and sunburst yellows. The suffrage flag with four gold stars on a blue background waved above the rest. The stars represented the four states that had already granted women the right to vote: Utah, Idaho, Wyoming, and Colorado.

Catt presided over the convention as the president of NAWSA with Rev. Shaw as vice president and Blackwell as recording secretary.[17] Low whispers, an occasional cough, and the swishing of skirts echoed in the sanctuary as Catt introduced guest speaker Barton.

The audience focused on women's suffrage, but issues of a legal and economic nature were also discussed, such as the disparity in wages for men and women in similar occupations. International commentary filled the afternoon and evening sessions, during which Emmy addressed the general assembly, once again recalling the suffrage movement in Sweden:

> I stand before this legislative power of America representing a country where women have voted since the eighteenth century, sanctioned in 1736 by the king.
>
> Women vote for every office for which their brothers do and on the same terms, except for the first chamber of the *Riksdag*. They have the municipal and school suffrage, votes for the provincial representatives, and thus indirectly for members of the House of Lords.[18]

She continued to point out that in Sweden, women and men working in the government received equal pay for equal work and that women could hold any job they wanted except for clergy. In addition, she told the audience that in 1809, women were given the rights of inheritance and equal matrimonial rights. Swedish colleges and universities accepted women students, allowing them to receive the same degrees as men.

In her final remarks, Emmy went on to say:

> You cannot trust the ballot to women who are controlling millions of dollars and helping support the country, but you give it to loafers and vagabonds who know nothing, have nothing, and represent nothing. You cannot trust the ballot in the hands of women who are the wives and daughters of your heroes, but you give it to those who are willing to sell it for a glass of beer. . . .[19]

Never one to mince words, Emmy expressed the truth with sincerity.

* * * *

Activities, speeches, and other gatherings filled that week as the women conducted a second conference. The International Woman Suffrage Conference ran simultaneously with the NAWSA meeting and required an invitation. The Fredrika Bremer Association, a Swedish organization working for gender equality, nominated Emmy to represent them at the convention. Women from eight other nations—England, Australia, Norway, Germany, Russia, Chile, Turkey, and the United States—also participated. Emmy happily made the motion that Anthony chair the conference.

Meetings opened with a prayer and a hymn, and formal addresses continued throughout the week. Emmy took the platform on Sunday, February 16, at eight in the evening on behalf of her Swedish sisters. While Emmy offered up Sweden as the foremost example of women's rights, she realistically pointed out that the laws were not consistently in favor of women.

> Women serve on school boards, boards of guardians of the poor, and parochial boards. A woman is free to choose her husband, and is permitted to marry at seventeen, but is required to have the consent of her tutor if she is not of age (twenty-one years).

> Unmarried women and widows have full property rights. She is the mistress of her earnings and collects and controls her own wages.

> Concerning divorce and adultery and the penalty attached, in most cases the statutes make no difference between a male and a female lawbreaker.

> They have a right to follow any trade or business, but a married woman must have the consent of her husband, who makes himself responsible for her liabilities. . . .[20]

During the international proceedings, Emmy served on a subcommittee with Anthony, Catt, and other delegates. Together they wrote a declaration that concluded that men and women were born *equally* free and were independent members of the human race who were *equally* endowed with talents and intelligence and *equally* entitled to exercise their individual rights. They called for relationships between the sexes that fostered interdependence and cooperation.

In addition, they proclaimed that existing laws were restrictive and unjust, and that in a modern society, no woman should owe obedience to a man. Furthermore, they considered taxation without representation to be tyranny because it denied women the right to "life, liberty, and the pursuit of happiness" as found in the Declaration of Independence.[21] They understood the word "people" as found in the document to be generic and not just pertaining to males.

* * * *

The delegates hurried about throughout the week, bracing against the cold. Emmy, who had already participated in the NAWSA and international conferences, prepared to speak before members of the US House of Representatives and the Senate. First on the docket, Catt took the floor and explained to a select committee of the US House of Representatives that delegates from the International Woman's Suffrage Conference would discuss suffrage in their respective homelands.

Vida Goldstein from Australia spoke first. Sofja Levovna Freidland from Russia followed. Emmy presented third. Wearing a long black dress with a high neck and ruffled front, Emmy, now forty-five years old, gave up the corkscrew curls of her youth for a more mature topknot. Her figure had filled out on her petite frame. Her speech illustrated the individual rights and opportunities for women in Sweden. Catt introduced Emmy by saying, "It is eminently proper, Mr. Chairman, that following Madam Friedland, Mrs. Emmy Evald, of Sweden, should address you, for the women of Sweden have voted longest of any women in the world."[22]

> Mr. Chairman and gentlemen, here I stand before this legislative power of America, representing a country where women have voted since the seventeenth century. . . . [Swedish women were granted conditional suffrage in the eighteenth century.]
>
> The Swedish women stand as the first women who have been granted enfranchisement, for Swedish women voted before any American man ever voted; and this striking fact is unquestion-

ably due to the liberal sentiments which Swedish men entertain for women themselves as well as for their cause. . . .

The men gave suffrage to the Swedish women without the women requesting it, because they believed that taxation without representation is tyranny. . . .

So, you see this movement for women's rights is greatly needed here. You cannot trust the ballot into the hands of women teachers at the public schools, but you give it to men who cannot write! I am sorry that my time is up, Mr. Chairman, as there are a number of other things I would like to call to your attention.

We hail the day and hopefully look to the future when American women will be declared equal to men judicially as well as socially, as citizens, and as human beings.

—Emmy Evald[23]

Soul-stirring and imbued with passion, Emmy's voice once again declared the inequities between the sexes.

Isabel Campbell pointed out that women's suffrage in her home state of Wyoming had existed since 1869, before it entered the union and with great results. This achievement contrasted the belief that equal suffrage would increase family discord and divorce rates or that the excitement of the political fray would cause nervousness, leading to insanity among the fairer sex. Two other women talked, one from Idaho and the other from Colorado, which allowed women to vote in 1893 followed by Utah in 1895 and Idaho in 1896.[24]

Catt and Florence Fenwick Miller of England closed the hearings. Catt requested that transcripts of the proceeding be sent to the floor of the House, and with the banging of the gavel, the meeting adjourned at 11:40 a.m.[25]

* * * *

The women scurried back and forth between the House and the Senate that day, proposing an amendment to the Constitution granting all citizens the right to vote regardless of their gender.

Fifteen delegates gave brief but impassioned speeches before a US Senate committee. Anthony began by reminding the men that women had come before seventeen Congresses over the past thirty-three years on the issue of suffrage. Blackwell cited Abigail Adams's remarks to her husband, President John Adams, asking him to consider "the ladies" as the men drafted new laws for an independent nation.[26]

Tireless, Emmy energetically delivered her speech to the Senate committee that morning. She reiterated much of what she had said in earlier speeches and concluded with these final remarks:

> You say that women are inferior, and you cannot give them the ballot, but your law says that you consider bad women equal with men and you mete out the same punishment for them. Would you deny to women the privilege of paying taxes? If they were murderers, would you know any difference in the law between the man and the woman! . . .
>
> You have not trusted the ballot in the hands of Mrs. McKinley simply because she is a woman, but you do trust it in the hands of anarchists.
>
> So, men, let justice speak and may the public will demand that this disenfranchisement of the noble American women shall be stopped. My heart cries for justice for these American women. I am sure that you men are ashamed of your laws. . . .
>
> A well-known American judge, attempting to convince a fugitive slave that he had made a mistake—this was before your Civil War—put the following questions to him:
>
> "What did you run away for?"
>
> "Well, Judge, I wanted to be free."
>
> "You had a bad master, I suppose."
>
> "Oh, no; berry good massa."
>
> "Well, you hadn't a good home?"
>
> "Haven't I? You should see my pretty cabin in Kentucky."

"Had to work hard?

"Oh, no; a fair day's work."

"If you had plenty to eat, was not overworked, had a good home, and a good master, I don't see why on earth you wanted to run away."

"Well, Massa Judge, I spec de situation am still open if you would like it." [Laughter.]

The judge saw the point and gave the fugitive a $5 bill to help him on his way to freedom. [Applause.]

I think we women suffragists feel something like this fugitive slave. If you ask us, "What in the world do the women want the ballot for?" we'd reply, "Oh, men, because we want to be free."

But further than that, our situation is open for you, Senators and Representatives of America, if you would like it. [Applause.][27]

Rev. Shaw followed Emmy as the last speaker of the morning. The group adjourned at 11:55 a.m. Chairs scooted as the women and the senators filed out of the room, muttering to themselves and commenting on the morning's events.[28]

At the close of the International Woman's Suffrage Conference, the women praised Anthony for her leadership and wished her a happy eighty-second birthday. Her white hair parted in the middle, Anthony fought back tears of gratitude with her strong chin trembling. Catt, a petite woman wearing a long dark fitted dress and jacket, received a lovely silver card case in appreciation of her efforts.[29]

Afterward, a writer for the *Washington Times* penned a fine commentary regarding the convention, saluting the women for their faith, ability, and interest in public affairs and lauding Anthony and the association for their vigor and uniqueness. The writer went on to say, "There was very little empty rhetoric but a good deal of fun. In short, there are two extra senses with which most of the delegates seem to be provided—common sense and a sense of humor—excellent substitutes for emotion when it comes to practical affairs."[30]

* * * *

Back home in Illinois other initiatives pushed forward. The thirteenth annual IESA convention in the Edgewater area, a lakeside community just north of Chicago, included communiqués from local clubs. Emmy's college chum and IESA president, McCulloch, addressed the group. Emmy gave a speech simply titled "Progress," and served as the superintendent of the "Work Among Foreign Women" department. An aging Anthony appeared as the guest of honor and featured speaker.[31] One account suggests Anthony stayed with Emmy when she visited Chicago.

The fight for equality continued at the annual Illinois state convention in Joliet on October 6–7, 1903. The women greeted each other and chatted briefly as they entered the room. The morning session opened with the usual business, treasurer's report, committee reports, and various speeches. Two topics of discussion came to the floor: "Should Tax Paying Be a Qualification for Admitting Women to the Ballot?" and "Should an Educational Qualification for Suffrage Be Applied to Women?" Emmy's address, as president of the International [Lutheran] Woman's League, came that afternoon.[32]

Following an evening banquet, several well-known women addressed the crowd, including Rev. Shaw and McCulloch, who had been described as "an ardent suffragette, [and] clever lecturer . . . no dowdy . . . she is daintily dressed and bright eyed."[33] McCulloch acknowledged that the Bible did not grant women the vote but argued that Eve's actions in the Garden of Eden did not require women to live a life of servitude.[34]

The women made little progress in the Prairie State during the next five years despite a supreme effort by Emmy and her companions. In 1907, McCulloch and her husband, Frank, led a group to Springfield as part of the IESA's campaign for municipal suffrage. With them were advocates from the Chicago Teacher's Federation, the WCTU, and Emmy's group, the Lutheran Woman's League.[35]

Women from all walks of life, from the well-to-do to the working class, took note. Of course, not every woman wanted the vote. In opposition to the powerful IESA, another group formed—the Illinois Association Opposed to the Extension of Suffrage.

In 1909, a special suffrage train ran from Chicago to Springfield in hopes of a triumphant win. The women also conducted road trips around the state to foster their cause. McCulloch helped organize a motor tour of the state in July 1910. Two automobiles carrying members of the IESA journeyed through fifteen Illinois towns. The women were instructed to pack light; after all, they had business to conduct. Their purpose was far more important than fashion, McCulloch instructed the women, "There are more important matters before us today than whether a woman should speak veiled or unveiled, whether she should wear jewels or not, and whether her hair should be braided or not. . . ."[36] Emmy and her suffragist sisters, who rallied hundreds of women, began to feel hopeful that the fight could be won.[37]

* * * *

By 1912, the voice of the suffragists grew louder despite their repeated failures. Imagine a society where adult sons wrote legislation governing their mothers. Politicians found the suffragists impossible to ignore. They had clearly demonstrated that they were not the weaker sex, mentally or physically, and were perfectly capable of mounting a campaign and raising money for it.

Emmy and her comrades won a milestone victory in the Illinois house and senate in June 1913, but not without protest from the "antis." The bill, which the public referred to as the Illinois Bill, granted women the right to vote in presidential elections. The landmark legislation made Illinois the first state east of the Mississippi River to ratify such a bill.

There were limitations, however. Women could not vote for Illinois state senators or representatives or for governor. They also had to use separate ballots and ballot boxes. Catt called their success "astounding."[38] The legislation turned the tide for the women's movement and marked a huge step toward winning national enfranchisement, not to mention that Illinois now had a total of twenty-nine electoral votes. Because electoral votes are apportioned based on the number of representatives and senators, which are, in turn, based on the total voting population, adding women as voters increased the electoral strength of Illinois.

Emmy accompanied Catt to the Mississippi Valley Conference in Minneapolis in May 1916. There Catt divided the "antis" into three categories: the conservatives, the pessimists, and the spoilers. The latter group were the real opponents to women's suffrage who used their wealth to influence legislators.[39]

* * * *

Participation in the suffrage movement began well before World War I, and millions more hopped on the bandwagon between 1900 and 1917, driving the movement forward. But they needed approval from the White House, and President Woodrow Wilson, who considered himself a progressive reformer, failed to commit to the cause.

When the war broke out, criticisms of the government were deemed unpatriotic. The suffragists turned their attention to helping the war effort and conducting a different sort of campaign, that of food and energy conservation. As such, the Evalds were expected to lower their thermostats to save coal. Homemakers were urged the use corn over wheat and to conserve meat, fat, and sugar.

Fruit pits and nut shells were recycled and made into gas masks. In doing so, the family demonstrated their love of country and cooperation with the government. President Wilson eventually urged Congress to amend the US Constitution to allow women to vote.

The war ended in 1918 and Americans celebrated. In 1920, Emmy and her compatriots had another cause for excitement. Illinois emerged as the first state to approve the Nineteenth Amendment granting women the right to vote. On February 14, 1920, NAWSA, whose membership had mushroomed, celebrated in the gold room at the Pick-Congress Hotel on South Michigan Avenue in Chicago. Emmy may not have attended the event. Her daughter Lillian gave birth that day to a granddaughter and her namesake, Emmy Charlotte Carlson. However, McCulloch and Catt were among the attendees at the hotel. Catt, recognizing the value of a women's organization, proposed a unique idea—the League of Women Voters.

The Nineteenth Amendment was ratified on August 18, 1920, seventy-two years after the early suffragists met in Seneca Falls, New York. Emmy at age sixty-three could vote. Women in Illinois would wait another nineteen years until 1939 before they could legally serve on a jury in that state.

While the Nineteenth Amendment allowed Emmy and many others to vote, it did not extend this right to all women. Due to certain laws and customs, African American women and other women of color were still disenfranchised. Native Americans gained the right to vote in 1924 (for some states, not until decades later); Asian Americans in 1952; African Americans in 1965; and non-English speakers in 1975.

Emmy lamented that some women seemed unconcerned about voting, which she declared as a great privilege. "I wish something could be done to awaken their sense of responsibility," she said. The number of women who were ill-informed about politics bothered her, because she viewed the knowledge of policymaking and legislation as essential to one's career.[40]

* * * *

On Emmy's eightieth birthday, McCulloch penned the following to her dear friend:

> There will be others who will talk about . . . your many services for charity. If I were only there, I would tell them about how helpful you were in everything good in Chicago and how you would go to Springfield and to Washington to help us secure the votes for women, always holding up to the congressmen and the legislators what Sweden had done for its women and urging the men of the United States to do as well.

> No one can measure the influence of one's speech, but you made many speeches on that subject on behalf of our American women, and I hope that the women who are present today will remember that they owe to you not only constant help and inspirations in

religious and missionary work, but they owe to you some of the freedom which they as American citizens experience in our great country.[41]

The fight for women's right to vote succeeded thanks to a group of valiant women. Such feminine outcries would not be heard again until the 1960s and 1970s, when women fought to enter male-dominated careers, to establish credit in their own names as married women, and demanded equal pay for equal work.

Chapter Five

The Woman's Missionary Society
(1892–1935)

The Woman's Missionary Society (WMS) epitomized the "modern missionary movement," in which mainstream Protestant denominations began forming mission boards in the nineteenth century. They intended to recruit volunteers to carry out the work of the church and underwrite mission projects. While several such organizations existed, the most outstanding may have been the WMS of the Augustana Synod.

The society formed in 1892 when several wives and lay delegates accompanied their husbands to the annual synod meeting in Lindsborg, Kansas. At the gathering, Emmy and a small group of pastors' wives assembled to establish an organization. They agreed upon the name "The Woman's Home and Foreign Mission (WH&FM) Society, which was later shortened to the WMS. To succeed, the society would need to be supported by faith, energy, proven ability, and . . . money.

Practically speaking, the leadership recognized that many of the members would not be able to travel to annual conventions. Therefore, they patterned the organization to complement the synod, with an annual national conference, district meetings, and local auxiliaries. The women envisioned a sister organization that would coordinate with other synod boards. In doing so, they hoped to foster excitement for mission projects in the United States and abroad.

Emmy served as president of the society, a position she maintained for forty-three years. Her job, although rewarding, came with challenges and disappointments. At the onset, there were fifty female members. Women paid the paltry sum of fifty cents in annual dues. Lifetime memberships cost ten dollars.[1] The income paid for mission work, literature, and administrative expenses. What started as a rivulet with a small and almost obscure beginning, became a mighty river forming tributaries which flowed across the land and into distant countries.[2]

"One shouldn't expect great things," said reporter Anabel Parker McCann of the *New York Sun*, "but fifty cents . . . built a chain of schools, hospitals, dispensaries, chapels, churches, boarding schools, dormitories and homes reaching around the world through China, India, Palestine, Africa and the United States and Canada, every one of which is a center of continuing service to humanity."[3]

The WMS remained a natural outgrowth of women's roles in the home, where they managed family budgets and organized household tasks. Within the organization they learned how to buy and sell property and gained hands-on experience running a non-profit organization.[4] In addition, single women could travel overseas where they could realize medical careers—professions from which they were excluded at home. Married women could work outside the United States alongside their missionary husbands. Both the organization and the people they served benefited. In short, the WMS allowed women to accomplish more as a group than any one person could do on her own.

Emmy was a dynamo of energy, ideas, and actions, which have rarely been paralleled. She made every attempt to include young people in the work of the church by involving them in fundraising programs. Textbooks in English and Swedish highlighted the mission fields in hopes of training future disciples for Christ from an early age. As president, she regarded herself as a "tool in her Master's service," and as such, believed that women had a special calling to spread the "good news" of the Bible. She noted the risen Lord first commissioned a woman to proclaim the news of the resurrection and that he spoke his first words to a woman in John 20:15–18.[5]

The nineteenth century, called "The Women's Century" in missionary circles, recognized women had a duty to help their sisters in foreign lands.[6] Emmy felt American women owed a debt to these women, who were enslaved and degraded in harems as well as those kept in purdahs, where women lived behind screens or veils and were required to cover themselves in public. Conventional wisdom suggested these practices kept the fairer sex fully dependent on their husbands. Emmy also presumed that the spirits of Chinese women were bound and dwarfed identical to their feet and voiced her opinion on the matter:

> It is the responsibility of Christian women to "go and tell" [the good news]. We live in terrible times . . . when vice, white slavery, and all evil has banded together in powerful organizations. We are compelled to meet organized evil with organized good. Women must organize for more effective work in combating all these evils.[7]

Her call to action shone like a beacon in a storm, and the WMS grew in numbers and in donations. By 1906, the rolls swelled to five hundred and the treasury exceeded $24,000.[8] More money and a growth in membership meant greater progress for the WMS. As the organization grew, they needed a communications vehicle to keep its membership informed. The WMS printed its first newsletter in 1906 and named it *Mission Tidings*. (Its original name in Swedish read *Missions Tidning*.) Emmy referred to the faithful messenger as "a little drop of ink." Subscriptions sold for twenty-five cents to be affordable for all. Sales were brisk that first year and provided enough money to cover the publishing costs.

"A woman's missionary paper was almost unheard of at the time. It was, therefore, with fear and trembling that our little paper made its appearance. It almost apologized for its existence," said newspaper editor Alma Swensson. "The need of a missionary periodical whose purpose is to make known the work of the organization it represents was clearly in evidence. . . . The information gives us inspiration. . . ."[9]

The publication included articles regarding the mission fields, updates on local activities, annual conferences, and financial statements, taking precautions to ensure that they did not overstep their bounds or conflict with other journals within the synod. Members viewed the tabloid as a success and welcomed it in their homes.

To alleviate any concerns, the purpose of the communications clearly stated it would not be used as a platform for women's rights. However, it did print such slogans as:

> The thermometer of a man's character is his attitude toward women.
>
> It is woman who is the measure of civilization.
>
> Women's status determines to a very large extent the character of her nation.

In time, the publication went from an eight-page quarterly to a monthly newsletter, and subscriptions topped at 1,800. Because younger WMS members were not fluent in the mother tongue, they added an English section. To satisfy the needs of her readers, Emmy made the following plea: "At our annual meeting, it was decided that our *Mission Tidings* be equally divided half in Swedish and half English. I will try to comply with this request, provided you will, dear young women, help me with your suggestions and use these columns as your medium of self-expression."[10]

Swensson edited the Swedish section and May Mellander the English. Emmy wrote two popular columns: Among Ourselves and *Syskonkretsen* ("Siblings"). Subscribers often turned to Emmy's columns before reading anything else.

Although the average woman might be satisfied with the achievements of the WMS, Emmy thought more could be done. Despite its success, she wanted the organization to be completely autonomous. From its beginning, the WMS worked under the auspices of the men's foreign mission board. In 1907, Emmy petitioned the General Council of the Lutheran Church and requested that the WMS be allowed to collect and disburse its own funds. Half of the money would pay for hospital equipment and staff in India. The remaining cash sponsored Chinese missions.

In her argument, Emmy observed that women made up half of the church rolls and that they labored faithfully on behalf of the church raising money for mission endeavors. But not one female served on a mission board. Her request was nothing short of extraordinary, given a woman's current position in society.

Emmy presumed Christian women could better appreciate the complexities of human suffering and degradation of their fellow sisters, and consequently, should be charged with their care. After much discussion, the men agreed, and the women remained in control of their own resources for decades.

Next was the matter of $12,000 that the WMS had raised for a hospital in Rajahmundry, India. Emmy wanted the WMS Executive Board to approve the building plans and anything else connected to the hospital. Furthermore, she requested that future management of the hospital be solely under the control of the WMS. To justify her cause, she cited the women-managed hospital in Guntur, India, as proof that the WMS could handle the task. Given the great need for the hospital, the synod agreed, and the women applauded Emmy for gaining control of the WMS disbursements.[11] Coincidentally, the Guntur Hospital, which was not a part of the WMS, closed its doors within three years due to lack of income.

Greater independence brought more opportunities. The society's women were both creative and industrious when devising fundraising schemes. They often exceeded their financial targets by employing several different ideas. "Blessing" boxes were quite popular, for example. Members put their box in prominent locations, such as above the kitchen sink, as a visible reminder of the blessings they had received. If something occurred during the day for which they were grateful, they would drop a coin into the box, thereby increasing the value of God's gift.

The WMS also produced educational and promotional materials for mission-related projects. Colorful postcards illustrating the harsh living conditions of people in different lands sold for a penny or more. Pamphlets in hues of pink, blue, and beige promoted the WMS activities. Coin books with slots for one dollar's worth of dimes were mailed by the thousands to raise money for foreign missions. Filling the books was not required by WMS members, but it was considered an honor to make a small donation to such a worthy cause. In addition, the society held prayer days on the first Sunday of Advent.

Calendars, which were largely Emmy's creation, sold for the low price of twenty-five cents and advertised mission work. The WMS touted the 1919 edition as the most desirable and interesting calendar ever issued with "valuable information that could not be obtained anywhere else."[12]

By 1916, WMS membership had reached fourteen thousand. Illinois was the largest district with nearly four thousand members, followed by Minnesota and Iowa. Throughout the society's history, goals were met, membership increased, newsletter subscriptions grew, and contributions continued. The Silver Jubilee Celebration in 1917 exemplified these efforts. WMS members set out to secure ten additional members, ten more subscribers and one lifetime member, or a gift of ten dollars.[13]

The two-year membership drive netted twenty thousand members and $30,000 in donations.[14] The constant call for money might have easily weakened the membership's resolve to donate more. The remedy for these feelings was to count their blessings and conclude that because they had received freely, they should give freely.[15]

* * * *

When war broke out in Europe, Americans hoped the United States would not be drawn into the conflict. However, with the sinking of the *Lusitania* by a German submarine, sentiments changed, and the country entered the "Great War" in 1917. Young men were drafted into the military, while others volunteered to fight. On the home front, Americans were expected to show their patriotism. Citizens mobilized to produce food and ammunitions. Food conservation initiatives called for "meatless Tuesdays," "wheatless Wednesdays," and "porkless Saturdays" to provide meals for the troops and nourishment for war-torn families overseas. Women took on men's jobs in the factories, and American homemakers economized and planted vegetables in "victory" or "war" gardens.

Schools and churches promoted patriotism. The Lutheran Church was especially patriotic. About 7.7 percent of its members—a greater proportion than any other mainstream religion—served in the war.[16]

The WMS followed suit with messages printed in the *Mission Tidings* newsletter, such as:

> Christian patriotism keeps the glow in Old Glory.
>
> Uncle Sam calls us to "Win the War." Buy war bonds.
>
> There must be no slackers among our ranks.

The publication printed messages from President Wilson and highlighted children of WMS members who served in the war. Its memorial page included an honor roll of WMS "Gold Star" mothers whose children had died in service of their country.

Thousands of young men from Augustana College and Theological Seminary enlisted in the armed forces, including scores of pastors who joined up as chaplains or camp pastors.[17] The war hit close to home for Emmy, whose son-in-law Rev. Hoffsten and nephew Corporal Egbert Carlsson were featured in the newsletter. Rev. Hoffsten served as a chaplain at Camp Grant outside Rockford, Illinois. Corporal Carlsson was a doughboy, a nickname for those who fought in the infantry in Europe, because their buttons resembled doughnuts.

The WMS newsletter also published articles about the Red Cross and war relief efforts, including a $7,500 contribution from the society for a field kitchen in France. The horse-drawn wagon, which resembled an early version of today's food trucks, provided hot coffee, doughnuts, and pie for the soldiers, giving them a taste of home and raising morale. When Emmy inquired as to what other items were needed, the reply from the military suggested baseball paraphernalia for the men stationed near the base hospitals.[18] Whether the request was filled is unknown.

The heaviest fighting in Belgium and northern France left thousands of orphans and fatherless families living in poverty in those countries. Women across America, including the WMS, took special notice. As mothers themselves, they eagerly reached out to aid the children. In 1918, the WMS declared the month of September as Lutheran Woman's War Drive. In keeping with the drive, the newsletter asked members to pledge money to aid the war's half million orphans in France. Emmy's plan included an even greater commitment, which she expressed in the newsletter: "Our paper wishes to do 'her bit' and will drop the September issue as a war conservation measure to help the dear little homeless war orphans."[19]

She proposed an idea in which to use the hundred-dollar savings to print pictures of war orphans in upcoming issues that, in turn, would generate interest and donations. A donation of thirty-six dollars helped a mother support her child for a year, but that was a lofty sum for women in 1918. For one hundred dollars, an even steeper cost, the WMS could "adopt" a war orphan, giving the child a home, education, and care.[20]

Because of Emmy's suggestion, the WMS sponsored fifty orphans and sent more than one thousand pounds of clothing. Additional donations were used to build and maintain homes for post-war orphans.[21] One widow from Montana was so struck by the forlorn photos of young children that she gave twenty-five dollars when she herself could barely make ends meet.[22]

The outpouring of support was overwhelming. A grateful Emmy penned the following message:

> In these past years, the *Mission Tidings* newsletter has greatly multiplied its usefulness. Each worker interested in our society can testify to its worth. It is a great transmitter and transformer of our work and our aim. Think of all who have heard the cries and helped the women and children in the world.[23]

Emmy's "little drop of ink" communicated the needs of others for decades to come, and the women of the Augustana Synod continued to help the less fortunate.

* * * *

At the fortieth annual WMS convention held at Immanuel Lutheran Church, the women reelected Emmy as president. In addition, they reaffirmed their support of prohibition, praising

President Herbert Hoover and other "dry" leaders for enforcing the National Prohibition Act, known as the Volstead Act.

Much of the meeting focused on mission efforts within the Augustana Synod. The greatest need was for trained teachers, nurses, and doctors. The society, with Emmy's blessing, determined that the best way to serve those less fortunate was to recruit and train women to serve in the mission fields and set out to do so. In response, the women raised thousands of dollars each year for missions in India, China, Africa, Puerto Rico, and the Holy Land. The donations provided missionary salaries, compensation for female doctors, and financial assistance for medical training when doctors were unavailable. Remarkably, Emmy even paid off the budget deficit for the men's mission society, for which the general council commended her.[24]

One of the first mission fields supported by the WMS occurred in Rajahmundry, India, approximately three hundred miles outside the state capital of Hyderabad. Rajahmundry existed as a part of the Madras Province before India's war of independence from Great Britain in 1947. The traditional class or caste system determined a Hindu's station in life, occupation, and social interaction with others. At the top were Brahmins, or the scholars, followed by the Kshatriyas, public officials; Vaishyas, businessmen; and Shudras, unskilled workers. The untouchables, or Dalits as they are known today, were the lowest caste and thought to be unclean. A person's position was set at birth and could not be changed.

Men in higher castes customarily took several wives. These women were housed in harems or apartments, out of touch with the outside world and unable to pursue their own ambitions. As reported in the WMS newsletter, women of lower castes could be contracted into marriage as infants and were often enslaved. If their husbands died, they were not allowed to remarry. Hence, India had twenty-six million widows, of which more than two million were under the age of ten and nearly three hundred thousand were under the age of five.[25]

Charlotte Swensson, the first missionary financed by the WMS, arrived in India at the turn of the twentieth century and began working with the Indian population and sharing biblical scriptures with them. In time, they built training facilities, seminaries, and schools. While in school, students gained more than a basic education. Classes at the mission ended with a short prayer. At the end of class, the missionaries passed out cards to the students with pictures of Jesus and scripture readings written in Telugu, a native language of India.

In addition to religious instruction, the Indian women learned lace making. The goods were purchased by the missionaries and sent to the United States to be sold, which afforded the women a modest income to buy food and clothing as well as some upward mobility. To be admitted to class, students had to be neat and clean in their appearance with their hair combed. The well-defined rules gave the women a sense of pride in their workmanship, and they worked hard to prove their worth.[26] Their efforts were rewarded in increased sales as reported by missionary Ada Christenson in her letter home:

> To the President of the WMS of the Augustana Synod and Mrs. Emmy Evald,
>
> The year that has just closed has been a banner year for the Indian lace industry. This phase of our mission work has won many friends and workers during the year. To show how much it has grown I would just mention that sales for the 1910–1911 [years] were $138.08, sales for this year [1912] have reached the pretty sum of $556.76.[27]

How much the lace-making industry influenced the village women is undetermined. But surely the additional income brought greater hope to the community.

* * * *

The Rajahmundry mission also included medical staff. Dr. Betty A. Nilsson began her career as a teacher in Rockford, Illinois, before attending medical school. She arrived in India in 1908, where she connected with two other doctors, three nurses, and three teachers. The woman's society gave her $100 for clothing and travel expenses plus a salary of $500 a year. Consistent with other mission workers, she spent her first two years in the field learning the vernacular before taking on additional duties. For the next twenty-five years, Dr. Nilsson cared for the sick, taking occasional leaves of absence to raise money for the mission.[28]

An urgently needed hospital was built in Rajahmundry in 1911 with the help of the Augustana Synod and women of the Pennsylvania Ministerium. The hospital building featured a warm brick façade with arched walkways along the first and second floors of the main section and along the annex. The WMS later held a banquet to recognize Dr. Nilsson's contributions with eight hundred people in attendance and endowed a bed at the Rajahmundry hospital in her honor.[29]

The hospital's benefits went beyond medicinal. "Medical missions are breaking down the power of the witch doctor and their pagan religion," said Emmy, whose desire was to bring Christianity to other lands.[30]

In 1917 alone, more than 1,000 patients were treated at the hospital in Rajahmundry, with 1,400 surgeries performed. More than 6,600 new patients visited the hospital dispensary. Out of all the medical services provided, only 32 patients died, illustrating the excellent care patients received under less-than-ideal conditions.[31]

But more than brick and mortar were needed. With basic medical necessities lacking, the WMS took it upon themselves to provide the hospital with supplies. One enterprising group held a festival with Emmy as the featured speaker.

"We sometimes marvel at the youthful strength and energy of which she [Emmy] has always been in full possession, but she seemed to have more than the usual amount of this youthful quality last Thursday. She is able to 'fire' any group with her missionary zeal and interest."[32]

The group hoped to raise $140 to furnish a hospital ward. Whether they met their goal was not reported, but every effort was appreciated.

Dear Friends,

We feel your help in many ways and how it fills our hearts with joy as we read of those who are so willingly sacrificing to do this great work. Especially now we see the interest societies and individuals have in furnishing of the hospital.

—Amelia Eckardt, missionary, Kotagiri, Nilgiris, India[33]

Eckardt was one of many missionaries who wrote of their progress in the fields and whose stories were reprinted in the *Mission Tidings* newsletter. These "Briefs from India" told of the workers' experiences and often recounted the hardships surrounding the native people and the extreme conditions in which they lived. Lying along the seacoast within the Torrid Zone, the hot climate of Rajahmundry lingered nine months of the year with abundant rainfall, unlike the upland districts which experienced little rain.[34]

> My dear friend, Mrs. Evald,
>
> . . . The most enjoyable coffee-party I have ever attended was in a mud hut with [a] mud floor and one room, with six small children and poor, sick parents and they invited Dr. Woerner and me to coffee, served in a tin bowl, but with such thankfulness . . . for help they had received during a prolonged and severe illness.
>
> Loving greetings from,
> Betty [Nilsson], Rajahmundry[35]

Over the years, the villagers, who had so little, continued to accept assistance from the mission workers with grateful hearts.

* * * *

From April to June, temperatures in Rajahmundry rose into the nineties and above. The tropical heat and humidity were particularly oppressive for the staff, who lived in large tents, but nobody complained. When time allowed, they took sabbaticals in the hilly region of Darjeeling. Life was peaceful at seven thousand feet above sea level. The women could gaze at the grandeur of the snow-capped Himalaya Mountains or indulge in a short hike up the road for a view of Mount Everest.[36]

After toiling in the mission fields, the change in scenery was a welcome sight and an enjoyable respite from the heat, as Eckardt wrote in her letter to the society:

> To the dear friends of the Woman's Missionary Society of Augustana Synod,
>
> We have now been at this delightful place of Darjeeling in north India for six weeks. . . . It is interesting to be among these hardy people of the north. They are strong and robust, of a Mongolian type, with a touch of rosy spots on their cheeks, and their bright eyes and smiling countenances make you feel attached to them at once. The people are all busy, women are knitting and sewing and often one sees a woman carrying her little one tied on her back walking and knitting. . . .
>
> With hardy greeting to all the friends of the *Mission Tidings* . . .[37]

Changing temperatures affected the missionaries but were not their only concern. Occasionally, adventures on the plains of India required quick thinking by field workers and their servants. While the locals often called on the missionaries, not all visitors were welcomed. Eckardt tells of a frightening encounter:

> To the *Mission Tidings*:
>
> . . . When reflecting over some of the events . . . I thought to write and tell you how thankful I am. . . . I had invited Mrs. Werner and her husband for afternoon coffee. I was going back and forth from the storeroom, where we keep our supplies, getting out things. I reached for a fruit tin on the high shelf, and as I raised my arm, I heard a most unusual noise. I left everything and stepped back quickly. Then I saw something black crawling up the wall. I made no noise at all, but called my servant, and told him to look.
>
> "Oh Annam," he said, "it is a cobra."
>
> . . . What to do and how to get at it was a question, as the room was small and full of things. As soon as Mr. Werner came, there was a search, as it had slipped away out of sight. But Mr. Werner

with a stick gently moved the things about until he found it, but how to get at it? The room was too small, and all the bottles were on the shelf where it was hiding. . . .

Once more we lost sight of it, and as it was somewhat dark, we lit a light and Mr. W. discovered it coiled up in a small wooden box. He asked me if there was a bottom in the box, but I could not remember. He covered it over with other boxes and pulled it along so if it [the cobra] fell out, it would have fallen to the floor. But the bottom of the box was there, and the cobra was carried outside, without doing any harm and nothing was broken. . . .

Imagine our surprise when we found that the monster measured six feet.[38]

Despite the perils and hardships, the mission programs in India remained, although funding and volunteers were always in demand. Every so often, the weary missionaries wondered if their efforts were in vain. With plans of returning to the United States, Eckardt shared her thoughts with her friends back home:

Dear Friends of the *Mission Tidings*,

You have all read the needs, and we must have help soon if the work in some areas is to be kept up. There is not one missionary, as far as I know, in the field who has regretted that she or he has come. . . . We are plowing and preparing the soil, but the fruits thereof are slow to ripen. . . .

Thus far, the weather has been comfortable. We are still in the tent, but soon it will be too hot. My husband and I have decided to stay on the plains this year as we go home next year.[39]

After years of service, missionaries often returned to the United States to refresh their spirits and raise awareness of the work being done. Some opted to go back to the mission fields with renewed hope.

While establishing schools and hospitals were a large part of the society's mission efforts, the other was to evangelize. Converting women and children was paramount to the spiritual salvation of the Indian people, or so the missionaries thought.[40] Just as the first disciples proclaimed the good news of Jesus, the missionaries used every opportunity to spread their message to all who would listen. Letters from the field reflected scores of joyful Indian women who welcomed Jesus into their lives, although the actual outcomes were hard to measure.

Dear *Mission Tidings*:

> . . . I bid your readers salaam and begin at once to tell you about my day in Kovvur . . . that is just opposite Rajahmundry, with only the broad Godavari [River] separating us . . . Here they are happy and gather with eagerness. . . .

> We cannot read men's hearts, but if the expression of the countenance is an indication, we believe that there is heartfelt desire for the great salvation which is made known through Christ our Savior.

Very truly your friend,
S. E. Monroe, missionary, Rajahmundry[41]

One by one, Emmy authorized the purchase of three school sites in Rajahmundry for more than $2,000 in hopes of building Christian girls' schools.[42] Meanwhile, available resources helped to educate two native girls as mission assistants.

India's fight for independence marked a turning point for the missionaries serving in India. WMS's efforts slowed down after a young Mahatma Gandhi began leading nonviolent protests in a quest for the country's freedom. Given the nation's unrest in the fall of 1917, they stopped sending missionaries to India. However, a training school was established in 1918 at the Rajahmundry hospital with a class of seven women who were yearning to learn. There were fewer patients at the hospital at the time, but the number of outpatients treated at the dispensary increased.[43]

In December 1926, the WMS Executive Board sent Dr. Nilsson $10,000 to build the Charlotte Swensson Memorial Home. Swensson had been well regarded in the mission fields before her passing. The WMS wished to continue her work of bringing hope and spirituality to the local women. Some modifications to the building and dormitories were made to save space and money. The project was completed in 1927, but medical workers and volunteers remained in short supply.[44]

* * * *

After establishing missions in India, Emmy and others began looking for other opportunities within the Augustana Synod. After reviewing the needs in different locations, the WMS decided on the Honan province in China, which is now known as Henan. Regarding the Chinese endeavor, Emmy wrote a note of encouragement to the WMS:

> It is not your money, but the pouring out of your young womanhood in ministry to a hand that waits to be lifted. The hope of China is in educating the village. China needs the healing touch which opens the heart of village to the missionary who will take them to Jesus Christ.[45]

The population of Honan was roughly five hundred people per square mile, or about three million "souls" waiting for conversion. It was one of the largest provinces in the country and one of the last to allow missionaries. (Years earlier, missionaries had been met by knife-wielding natives.)

Located on the central plains, the area was about the same latitude as southern Oklahoma. The topography was diverse with mountains to the west, floodplains to the east, and the Yellow River flowing through it. At the time, the western section of the province between the mountains and the city of Juchow (now Juzhou) was notorious for bandits. Once the center of civilization, it had become the center of crime, where travelers were advised to arrive before dark and leave after daylight.

In 1905, Rev. August Edwins and his wife, Alfreda, were among the first missionaries to arrive. After learning the language and customs, the couple searched for a suitable spot to build a mission post. Having been attacked by ruffians earlier in their travels, they received a military escort and arrived safely in Hsuchow (now

Xuzhou), Honan, where they were united with Sister Ingeborg Nystul in 1906.[46]

Traveling was not an easy task. Only two mission centers— Hsuchow and Honan-fu (now Henan Prefecture)—had access to railroads. The others were reached by ox cart over bad roads.[47] Upon arrival in China, workers proceeded up the Yangtze River via a small steamboat, passing by fertile meadows and rocky cliffs. Mountains jutted upward in the distance, and fishermen sat quietly on the banks with their nets cast into the river, abundant with fish. Houseboats lined the shore appearing as small floating villages.[48]

Others went by junk, which was a Chinese vessel powered by sail or pulled by men along the Han riverbank. To lighten the load, the passengers would leave the junk and walk along the riverbanks.

> At nightfall, the junk would tie up to the bank, which was predicated by the local civil conditions, bandits, or strife. The master of the junk would decide which side was the safest based on word of mouth from the residents or down-stream boats. . . . we later called this means of communication the "bamboo telegraph."
>
> —David C. Edwins, missionary's son[49]

After traveling down river, the missionaries and their families continued their journey inland by train. The cramped aisles and wooden seats lacked the creature comforts of home, and luggage banged about the train car. The landscape changed from rural towns, where huts of golden straw resembled haystacks, to larger cities, which were dirty and crowded with people clamoring in every direction and vendors selling cakes and roasted meat along the narrow streets.[50] The trip was arduous but full of promise.

The final leg of the trip took the missionaries and their families up a rugged mountain path to their simple homes.

> Crude sedan chairs borne by coolies were our mountain taxis. . . . to reach our destination we had to ascend four miles of steep paths, including a stretch memorable for its one thousand stone steps.
>
> —Ruth Vikner Gamelin, missionary's daughter[51]

These early missionaries arrived with preconceived notions of life in China and found the conditions of their home to be better than expected—which is not to say that conditions were comfortable. The homes with dirt floors and walls of mud were cramped and lacked modern conveniences or privacy. Ceilings of bamboo mats provided racetracks for rats and blocked much of the sunlight.[52]

Honan's central location and proximity to the river caused flooding, while subtropical temperatures meant hot and humid summers and cooler winters. To escape the heat, the missionaries often took trips to the interdenominational mountain resort on the southern edge of the province.

The WMS under Emmy's direction procured the needed capital to pay the missionary staff and to purchase provisions, especially the sorely needed surgical towels, common pins, and bandages. Eventually, the society collected enough money to sustain teachers and doctors in the mission fields and provide financial aid to native workers and protégés. In addition, money was collected for a hospital at the Hsuchow mission station in 1911. During the worst times, makeshift beds were built between two poles to carry the sick. Men arrived by camels, severely wounded by bandits.[53]

More WMS missionaries came every year despite the dangers. Their numbers peaked at thirty-two in 1914. By 1919, hospitals opened in Honan-fu and Juchow, treating thousands of patients annually. Two schools were built—one for the blind in Honan-fu and another girls' school in nearby Kiahsien (now Jiaxian). Emmy took pride in the progress the mission efforts had made in education. The schools were now self-sufficient and self-directed. The WMS was also making plans for another high school and a training school for Chinese workers.[54]

"One of the greatest social changes in our history as a result of Christianity is that women have been taken from behind closed doors and set in the middle of the world," said Emmy.[55]

While the many advancements in China brought joy, there was also uncertainty. The missionaries in China also wrote of their experiences, which were reprinted in the *Mission Tidings* newsletter. In her "Letter from China," one missionary reported dirty, dark hovels in the village of Honan, with men and women clinging to their idols and superstitions. Others wrote of revolts and uprisings during the Chinese Revolution from 1911 to 1912, which resulted in the overthrow of the Qing dynasty, the last of the Imperial dynasties.

> Dear Friends,
>
> Almost like an earthquake came the revolution upon China last autumn, and thoroughly it has shaken the foundations of the vast country. Now after months of bloody battles and sorrow, starvation, and tears—as well as noble deeds done by patriotic Chinese heroes—peace and order are again returning. Golden stands the wheat fields promising a good harvest. . . .
>
> Yours in Christ's glad service,
Ingeborg Nystul, missionary, Honan[56]

That optimistic viewpoint did not last long. More than a year passed, and the situation deteriorated for the missionaries, who toiled under deplorable living conditions. Perhaps they wondered why the God they so faithfully served allowed such hardships in this war-torn country where dangers and bloodshed prevailed.

> Dear friends,
>
> . . . The suffering of the people here through war, famine and now the robbers, who are overrunning the land, has been sore. . . . Our mission property in Kiahsien is a long narrow strip. There are twelve buildings on the premises, divided up in six separate courtyards. The buildings, which are said to be over two hundred years old, were formerly a Mandarin's residence and are appropriately arranged for a mission station. . . .
>
> The joy of the Lord is your strength,
Thyra Lawson, missionary, Honan[57]

Living in Asia without the modern conveniences magnified the Chinese culture. After a few years in the field, some of the missionaries got homesick. Language studies helped ease their loneliness by allowing them to communicate better with the locals.

Nonetheless, Chinese customs seemed odd to the missionaries, who were greeted with a bow instead of a handshake. In the cities, luckless men worked as coolies carrying the well-to-do Chinese and outsiders. To ride in a jinricksha pulled around by a human being was strange indeed. To see coolies laboring as they pushed and pulled heavy loads stranger still.[58]

"More often four coolies worked as a team, coordinated by rhythmic chanting or singing that hummed in the background of our daily life. Coolie chants and a five-tone music scale were the sounds of our China," wrote Gamelin.[59]

Humans pulling carts resembling workhorses in America paled in comparison to other traditions. The Chinese custom of foot binding, which affected women's balance and inhibited their movement, was perhaps most difficult for the missionaries to understand. However, what was thought to be cruel by Western norms was an accepted Chinese practice and a sign of beauty among the women.

> When little girls reach the age of four, they must begin to have their feet bound. A bucket of water, as hot as can be borne, is produced. Into this the little girl must place her feet . . . to soften the joints and ligaments. Then the four smaller toes are bent backwards under the sole of the foot, which is then bound very tightly. The poor little girls scream as if someone were taking their lives. The Chinese say that for every pair of bound feet there is shed a whole bucket full of tears. . . .

—Alfreda Edwins, missionary's wife, Honan[60]

Western customs were equally confusing to the Chinese, and women came with questions of their own for the Americans. Why did the missionaries have rugs on the floor? Tablecloths? Sheets and a mattress? It was difficult to imagine the necessity of such items in a Chinese household where the floors were dirt and the family slept in a single room on woven mats. American habits were unusual, as was their physical appearance.

> One day while I crossed the road to go over to our school, some men passing by saw me and exclaimed, "Is that a man or a woman?" This just because my feet were so large. . . .

Many wondered why our hair is so light and not black like theirs. Some think that we must eat much rice and drink milk since our skin is so much fairer than theirs. . . .

—Alfreda Edwins[61]

Attitudes, traditions, and language were but a few of the obstacles to be overcome. Young Chinese girls learned to care for younger siblings, do housework, and bargain in the marketplace. The Chinese believed girls were not as valuable as boys, were not worth educating, and in some cases, were not as smart. Few women could read. But by all accounts, they had a thirst for knowledge, and public opinion was beginning to change.

Evangelism was equally as challenging. Confucianism, Taoism, and Buddhism were the prevailing religions at the time, leaving millions of Chinese in need of Jesus. Although the Chinese were too polite to point out any grammatical errors, spreading the gospel in a foreign language was difficult. Certain words or expressions were not found in a written language or were misinterpreted. Akin to farmers who toiled in the fields plowing, sowing, and reaping, so did the missionaries. Month after month, they tilled the minds of the people, planting hope and the Holy Spirit. They believed that the only thing that could lift women out of degradation, superstition, and ignorance, and bring them blessings, joy, and peace, was the good news of Jesus.[62]

Some evangelical efforts were less successful than others. Men often brought their wives to the mission stations proclaiming an interest in religion. What they really wanted was legal help in solving a personal matter.[63] Mission workers also wrote of the high rate of suicide among hapless women because of ill treatment and seclusion. Lawson was so concerned with the women's welfare that she sent an urgent request to the WMS for more "lady workers" to help stem the tide.[64]

When news of novelist Pearl Buck's criticism of foreign missions in China appeared in the *Chicago American* newspaper, Emmy, at age seventy-five, was unflappable. She acknowledged Buck's understanding of the Chinese culture and character but responded that Buck's repudiation of the divinity of Christ meant her charges were unfounded.[65]

While China was the largest of the mission efforts, work was carried out elsewhere. The WMS newsletter described efforts in Persia (now Iran) and the conditions of women secluded behind bars and living in harems with faces veiled. "A nation can be lifted no higher than its women are lifted," claimed Marie Telleen, Dr. John Telleen's wife.[66] Little or no education was provided to Persian women, and the selling of young girls as temporary wives was common. Schools, hospitals, and industries helped improve their living conditions with the hopes of leading them to Christ.[67]

"Women are born with cattle and die with cattle; they work hard in the fields, carrying their babes as well as their tools. They cut grain with one hand and gather it with the other hand. A working woman earns five cents a day. A laboring man makes twice as much," explained Emmy.[68] Her vivid description pointing to the differences between Persian women and those in the United States sparked contributions from WMS members.

Outreach programs in northwest Canada proved equally challenging. Vast open landscapes stretched from the US border to the lumber district and along the sound, forcing missionaries to travel great distances. The parishioners endured weeks without sunshine while heavy rain washed away roads, but they were undeterred. Sunday schools were full of multicultural children intent on learning the Gospel.

In Puerto Rico, efforts included the construction of a simple chapel near San Juan, whose Spanish Sunday school numbered seventy-five "bright and happy young people."[69] Donations also allowed for a mission home and missionary salaries. Lace-making projects were started with some notable results. The WMS also financed a missionary and buildings in the Holy Land. In 1922, work began in the Tanganyika Territory (now the Republic of Tanzania) in East Africa, the latest venture. There the Africans worked the fields with hoes planting corn, beans, or peanuts, while children tended the farm animals, making sure the cows did not graze in the planted fields. Six buildings were erected in the territory, four of which were hospitals that supplied health care for tens of thousands at the mission station.[70] The society also provided more than $14,000 in financial aid for the missionaries who lived there.[71]

Emmy was not content to live in the glory of her years as president of the WMS. Nor did she stop to reflect on the hope that she and the WMS brought to thousands of women around the globe.[72] Instead, she expanded her focus beyond far-off missions, directing her attention closer to home. She called on the members of the WMS to give more time and money, that is, "to look after the needy at our very doors."[73] Neglecting the home front, she feared, would cause remote missions to die. "If we can win our people for Christ, we will have both workers and means for our foreign missions," said Lorraine Peterson, member of the WMS Executive Board.[74]

Emmy set high standards for herself and expected the same from the staff and mission workers. She urged women, who now had gained the right to vote, to exercise their clout and help those who were still oppressed. "Throw the whole weight of your influence [resulting from] the Nineteenth Amendment," wrote Emmy in hopes of energizing the members of the WMS.[75]

She believed women could do anything if they believed in themselves. Her goal was to train as many women as possible for field work. They, in turn, could train others, thereby multiplying their efforts. By increasing the number of teachers, Emmy hoped to add more workers in God's service. After all, more teachers meant more progress in the mission fields.

Responding to the call of a Christian life was easier said than done. No two mission stations were the same. Each had unique challenges, delights, and difficulties. Where there appeared to be sunshine in one spot, dark clouds hovered over another. However, the missionaries persevered because they had one thing in common: dedication to providing years of service. Even when they felt the church "at large" had forgotten them, the missionaries continued to toil in the mission fields, each worker contributing to the growth of the church.

* * * *

In 1911, at the annual WMS convention in Lancaster, Pennsylvania, delegates voted to unify their operations by forming a national organization and pooling their resources. The women agreed that financial documents should be sent out twice a year. They also planned to establish a central location for publications and literature. However, this idea would not be realized for more than a decade, due to a shortage of cash.

With eighty-five districts, each with its own set of officers and department secretaries to carry on the work of the society, the WMS needed a location to call its own. The executive board currently met at the Immanuel Lutheran Home on LaSalle Street in Chicago, while May Mellander, literature secretary, and Alice Johnson, office secretary, worked from home. The situation called for a national headquarters where the work of the organization could be coordinated and redundancies eliminated.

At the 1923 annual convention in Rockford, Illinois, the women agreed to purchase a building to fulfill several needs. First, it would serve as WMS headquarters. Second, it would be home for missionaries returning on furlough. Finally, it would serve as a venue for social events and meetings. Such a building was located at 3939 Pine Grove Avenue in Chicago. With a down payment of $2,000 and a total cost of $40,000, the stately three-story red-brick building was purchased, much to Emmy's delight.

"There will be a dozen boxes and bushel baskets filled with various things that have been stored in my attic for years and other women have had suitcases and trunks in closets, storerooms, basements, and even in barns. Oh, what a help to have a common landing place," wrote Emmy. "It seems a dream. We got a brick house with fourteen rooms for land value." [76]

The multipurpose building was a blessing indeed. The first floor featured an executive office with four large windows. On warm days, cool breezes swept in from Lake Michigan. The living room, library, and dining room with its oak beams and fancy sideboard with cut-glass doors were also in the main floor. Off the dining room, the compact kitchen with its ample cabinetry was well-designed and saved multiple steps during meal preparation. Five large bedrooms and a sleeping porch were on the second floor. The top floor had an additional five bedrooms.[77]

Emmy's daughter Annie Hoffsten, followed by her granddaughter Ruth Hoffsten Mumford, turned out to be an able assistant at the Pine Grove location.

* * * *

As its longtime president, Emmy played a vital role, dedicating half of her life to the society without a salary or compensation of any kind while paying a goodly portion of her travel expenses. She tended to every department and detail, no matter how small, and often planned and oversaw important events. She attended annual conventions and made personal visits to the different districts within the organization. She handled correspondence from birthday wishes to financial matters, and wrote words of encouragement, or in the case of her nephew, a stern note admonishing him for ignoring his mother. Her letters were written on onion skin in English and Swedish. Occasionally her responses were delayed due to illness or a lack of time. If the inquiry required an immediate reply, she asked that it be sent via telegram. In addition to letter writing, Emmy submitted articles to the *Mission Tidings* newsletter for twenty-four years.

Over her lifetime, the WMS raised approximately $3 million for mission projects in the United States and abroad.[78] With the help of those who worked diligently on Emmy's behalf, the WMS provided education, health care, and news of God's kingdom to thousands of women from Asia's Pacific Rim all the way to the Pacific Coast of North America.

The WMS was Emmy's greatest lifetime achievement and the one for which she is renowned. With nearly sixty thousand members nationally, the society built seventy-four mission buildings: thirteen in the United States, thirty-eight in China, nine in Africa, eleven in India, two in the Holy Land, and one in Canada. The society also paid the expenses for thirty-four missionaries. Future endeavors were to be limited, however, to existing missions rather than the creation of new ones.[79] In the United States, funds helped to build churches in California and Nebraska. Lutheran residence homes provided affordable housing for missionaries and young women.

Now that the WMS was thriving, and the society owned a place to hang its hat, happy times should have prevailed. But in a few years, the relationship between Emmy and the WMS would begin to fray, posing her greatest challenge yet.

The Carlsson girls, Emmy (left) and Annie (right), at the Rostad School for Girls in Kalmar, Sweden, under the guidance of *Mamsell* Cecill Fryxell's school, ca. 1871.

As a young woman, Emmy began writing magazine articles on women's suffrage.

Emmy at Rockford Seminary in Rockford, Illinois, where she majored in voice, musical theory, and composition, ca. 1883. Her course of studies also included math, science, Latin, and geography.

Emmy and Carl Evald on their wedding day, May 24, 1883.

Rev. Carl Anderson Evald, whose talents in the pulpit were well known, was installed as the second pastor at Immanuel Lutheran Church.

The newly married Mrs. Emmy Evald. As a preacher's wife, she used the church to gain entrance into a man's world.

The parlor at 218 Sedgwick
in Chicago where the Evald
family lived.

Emmy and Carl Evald with their young children, Annie (left) and Lillian (right). As newlyweds, the Evalds started their family soon after their marriage.

Emmy and Carl with their school-aged children, Lillian (left) and Annie (right). Emmy once used her children as a subject for an oil painting.

SECOND EDITION.

THIRTIETH ANNUAL CONVENTION

OF THE

National American Woman Suffrage Association

AND THE

CELEBRATION OF THE FIFTIETH ANNIVERSARY OF THE FIRST WOMAN'S RIGHTS CONVENTION,

WILL BE HELD IN THE

COLUMBIA THEATRE, 12th and F Streets,

WASHINGTON, D. C.

February 13, 14, 15, 16, 17, 18, 19, 1898.

———

RELIGIOUS SERVICE, SUNDAY AFTERNOON, FEBRUARY 13, AT 3 O'CLOCK.

SERMON BY REV. ANNA HOWARD SHAW.

———

Day Sessions Free.
Evening Sessions, Silver Offering.
Reserved Seats, 25 cents additional, on sale at Theatre

Hotel Headquarters at "The Regent,"
15th St. and Penna. Ave.

Program from the thirtieth annual National American Woman Suffrage Association convention held in Washington, DC, in 1898. Emmy's speech on the work of Swedish women in America met with thunderous applause.

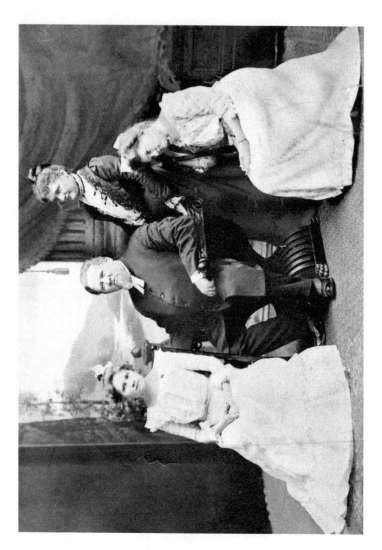

Emmy and Carl with their daughters, Annie (left) and Lillian (right), ca. 1897. The girls were a captive audience at Emmy's Bible classes held on Sunday afternoons.

Attendees at the International Woman's Suffrage Conference in Washington, DC, where the fight for equal rights persisted at the thirty-fourth annual NAWSA convention, February 12–18, 1902.

Front row (seated): Rev. Anna Shaw (second from the left); Susan B. Anthony (third from the left); Alice Blackwell, *Woman's Journal* (fifth from the left).

Back row (standing): Carrie Chapman Catt (fifth from the left); Emmy Evald (on the end).

The Evalds with their adult daughters, Lillian (left) and Annie (right), prior to Carl's death in 1909.

Emmy Evald, ca. 1910. As an orator of some renown, Emmy energized the WMS, adding to its membership.

Emmy and her companion, Mrs. Landstrom, traveling in an armored boxcar through the countryside during the Chinese Revolution. Soldiers shot at the insurgents on the ground, who fired back.

Emmy (front row, right) poses with her "little jewels" while visiting the mission schools in China in 1926.

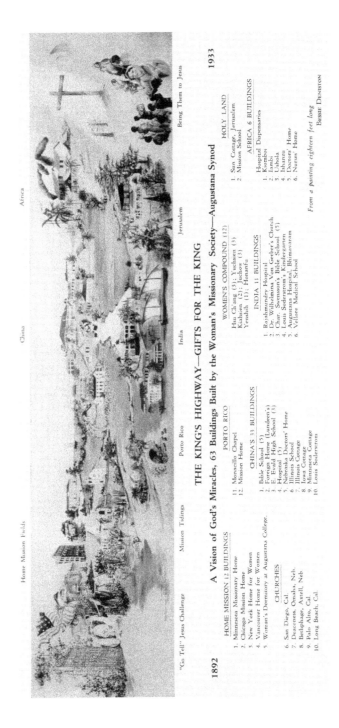

"Go Tell" Jesus Challenge   Bring Them to Jesus

1892   1933

THE KING'S HIGHWAY—GIFTS FOR THE KING

A Vision of God's Miracles, 63 Buildings Built by the Woman's Missionary Society—Augustana Synod

HOME MISSION 12 BUILDINGS

1. Minnesota Missionary Home
2. Chicago Mission Home
3. New York Home for Women
4. Vancouver Home for Women
5. Woman's Dormitory at Augustana College.

CHURCHES

6. San Diego, Cal.
7. Deaconess, Omaha, Neb.
8. Bethphage, Axtell, Neb.
9. Palo Alto, Cal.
10. Long Beach, Cal.

PORTO RICO

11. Monacillo Chapel
12. Mission Home

CHINA'S 33 BUILDINGS

1. Bible School (5)
2. Foreign Home (Lundeen's)
3. E. Evald High School (5)
4. Hospital (5)
5. Nebraska Doctors' Home
6. Illinois School
7. Illinois Cottage
8. Iowa Cottage
9. Minnesota Cottage
10. Louis Soderstrom

WOMEN'S COMPOUND (12)

Hsu Ch'ang (3); Yuchsien (3)
Kiahsien (2); Juchou (3)
Yenduh (1); Honanfu

INDIA 11 BUILDINGS

1. Rajahmundry Hospital
2. Dr. Wilhelmina Von Gerber's Church
3. Char. Svensson's Bible School (5)
4. Louis Soderstrom's Kindergarten
5. Augustana Hospital, Bhimavaram
6. Vellore Medical School

HOLY LAND

1. Sun Cottage, Jerusalem
2. Mission School

AFRICA 6 BUILDINGS

Hospital Dispensaries
1. Krombro
2. Jambi
3. Ushola
4. Ishanzu
5. Doctors' Home
6. Nurses' Home

From a painting eighteen feet long

BESSIE DENSTON

Illustration of the King's Highway, showing the buildings erected by WMS from 1892 to 1933.

WOMAN'S BUILDING

AT

AUGUSTANA

"God Bless the College That Keeps Our Daughter"

A Plea for Our Daughters

CAMPAIGN NOV. 6-20

A fundraising pamphlet encouraging donations to the woman's
building fund at Augustana College, Rock Island, Illinois.

Emmy with her children and grandchildren, ca. 1918. Emmy enjoyed taking the children to the Lincoln Park Zoo for picnics, pony rides, and ice cream.

Front row, from the left: Carl Hoffsten, Ruth Hoffsten (Mumford), Reynold Carlson, Emmy Evald, Burley Carlson (in Emmy's lap), Gertrude Hoffsten.

Back row, from the left: Annie Evald Hoffsten, Lillian Evald Carlson, Frances Hoffsten (Kern).

Emmy's home at 1453 Berwyn Avenue in Chicago in the summer of 1931. Emmy lived with the Carlson family and others in the 1920s and early 1930s.

(Left to right) Granddaughter Emmy, Daughter Lillian, and Grandson Reynold.

Emmy at work in her little niche at the Lutheran Home in New York City.

Emmy on her eighty-fifth birthday, September 18, 1942.
More than two hundred guests attended her birthday party.

Chapter Six

Triumphs and Turbulence (1920–1930)

A new era dawned, the Allies won the war, and Americans were experiencing a heyday of flappers and speakeasies, necessitated by Prohibition. Between World War I and World War II, a yawning gap grew between big city and rural life. Initially, a large portion of Chicago's population came from agricultural communities. But by the 1920s, residents were disconnected from the farm, and Swedish immigration slowed to a trickle.

Electrified traffic lights, painted lanes on streets, and changes in the law called for drivers to yield the "right of way." Carl Sandburg's poem titled "Chicago" referred to the city as the site of one thousand deadly street accidents. Livery stables were converted into garages, and teenagers discovered the "backseat."

Chicago was a new metropolis. Businesses relocated. Like a layer cake, one change—be it economic, cultural, or technological—affected the others. Skyscrapers were twice as tall, climbing forty to fifty stories. People traveled via the New York Central Railroad, an express train that departed Chicago at five in the evening and arrived in New York City within sixteen hours. The Vaudeville era of the 1880s gave way to theaters and radio programs, such as *Amos and Andy* and *Fibber McGee and Molly*. Live opera could be heard on station KYW in Chicago. New forms of music gained popularity and jazz clubs emerged. The city sizzled.

Autos and electrified rail transportation carried the population away from the city. Suburbia was born along with the Chicago bungalow, which offered affordable housing to the middle class. In contrast to the Victorian homes occupied by the wealthy, bungalows came with indoor plumbing. Courtyard apartment buildings built in a U shape provided grassy areas in the middle where children could play.

In 1921, Immanuel Lutheran Church moved from its Sedgwick and Hobbie location to the Edgewater neighborhood at Elmdale and Greenwood Avenues, where it remains today. The new Gothic-style building was constructed of brick and Indiana limestone. Three bells from the old church were laid on the front lawn as a reminder of Immanuel's illustrious history.

But booming prosperity had its seamy side. Thousands were involved in the illegal transportation and distribution of booze. The work was lucrative, organized, and dangerous. The Tommy gun, known as the "Chicago typewriter," and Al "Scarface" Capone led to Chicago's most notorious period of history and crime. The handshake murder, in which the victim's gun hand was tied up while a partner shot him, was quite effective. Capone was also known to use suitcase bombs and drive-by shootings. Although the streets were ablaze with gunfire, one battle had been won: women had gained the right to vote.

* * * *

As news of Emmy's achievements spread to Sweden, King Gustaf V sent his emissary, Consul von Dardel of Chicago, to present her with the distinguished Royal Vasa Medal of Honor, awarded in recognition of her outstanding work with the Swedish American people, her Christian service, and her involvement in the suffrage movement. The ceremony occurred in the Gold Room of the Auditorium Hotel on Michigan Avenue on January 10, 1922. Five hundred Swedish men and women attended, including family members and her longtime friend McCulloch.[1] Numerous speakers recounted her deeds, and huge applause resonated throughout the room as the medal was presented. For the occasion, Emmy wore a new black lace dress and had her photo taken with the medal pinned to her garment.

In her note of appreciation, Emmy praised her parents, and the WMS for its loyalty and wonderful response to service.[2] She then invited the banquet committee to her home for dinner, including the consul and his guests.

That year, the Swedish newspaper *Ailsvensk Samling* asked its readers to name the five greatest and most renowned Swedes living in other lands. Emmy's name topped the list[3]—proof, noted the newspaper, that Emmy was known the world over for her unselfish, untiring, and versatile labors, and especially, for her faith and Christian service to women around the globe.[4]

* * * *

As an excellent orator, Emmy often found herself in demand to speak before churches within the Augustana Synod and other organizations who sought her. On one occasion, while delivering an impassioned presentation at Augustana College and Theological Seminary, the waistband on her slip broke. Unfazed, she calmly stepped out of her lingerie, pushed it aside with her foot, and continued her oration.

She traveled extensively during the 1920s on behalf of the WMS despite her advancing age. Her close friend Mrs. John Linn usually accompanied her as she crisscrossed the country from the eastern shore of New York and Massachusetts to the plains of North Dakota and Nebraska and finally to the California coast. Emmy wrote the following about her trip in the *Mission Tidings* newsletter:

> October and November have been very busy months for me. While in Minnesota, I visited sixteen churches, spoke twenty-one times, and slept in eleven different houses. While at the Superior conference, I spoke twenty-eight times in twenty-three different churches and slept in twenty different homes. That is going some; it was quite a strenuous trip.[5]

Her excursions included international travel as well. In June 1923, Emmy sailed with her daughter Annie and her son-in-law Rev. Hoffsten to Paris as part of a world evangelizing mission. The trio headed home via Naples, Italy. Later that year, the WMS board paid a portion of her travel to Sweden in recognition of her thirty years of service. Her most daring adventure was a journey to China in the throes of a revolution.

* * * *

In 1924, the January weather forecast contained snow. Wieboldt's department store advertised hats on sale. New Year's horns sold at a bargain price of nineteen cents, and flapper styles were all the rage. But the gaiety surrounding New Year's celebrations gave way to a dark threat. The missions were under siege by Chinese bandits in the province of Honan. Local papers reported the murder and mayhem that befell the missionaries, including in the *Chicago Daily Tribune*, January 1, 1924:

> Massacres were reported in China by bandits near the Honan border, 400 miles from Hankow. Those who were murdered included an American woman from Northfield, Minnesota, and another man from Grand Forks, North Dakota, was wounded.

> Missionary reports stated that the same bandits raided the town of Likwanchiao and committed wholesale murder. The men, defending the place, threw their wives and children over the walls into a moat to avert a worse fate. The bandits finally took the town, slaying all the defenders.

That same year, two mission stations in the province of Honan at Kiahsien and Juchow were looted. Thankfully, the missionaries were unharmed. After the attack at Kiahsien, the staff fled to Hsuchow before returning a bit prematurely. Sister Nystual, a frequent correspondent for the WMS newsletter, and Sister Bergland, a teacher, were captured and tortured by bandits demanding money.[6] Whether or not they returned safely to the mission station is unknown.

* * * *

Revolution was not new to China. Throughout its history, the peasants had revolted against imperialistic regimes, which controlled industry and railroads and wielded great economic power. Warring factions spread violence, vying for power in the early twentieth century. The Boxer Rebellion from 1900 to 1901 began in opposition to imperialism and Christianity.

At the time, primitive and chaotic regional governments ruled China. In the years 1911–12, Sun Yat-sen toppled the Qing dynasty and founded the Republic of China. As China's first president, Sun founded the Kuomintang, or Chinese Nationalist Party, which grew politically and militarily. With the goal of unifying China, he set out to defeat the warlords who controlled the northern sections of the country. New centers of industry sprang up in the major cities of Shanghai and Hong Kong. New methods and subjects were introduced into classrooms in a desire to modernize the traditional Confucian educational system. But chaos raged, putting Christian missionaries at risk.

Along with his Russian connections, Mao Zedong, leader of the Chinese Communist Party, offered military aid to Sun. Although the Communist Party acknowledged the importance of Christian schools and modern education, the new sense of nationalism had disastrous effects for Christians, with mission outposts becoming targets. Undaunted, Emmy voiced her opposition to communism:

> The opposition is to Christianity not to Christ. The church is a foreign institution; Christ is their own. We must let them know that they can accept Christ and reject Western civilization and that they can separate the church organization from the Christian faith. . . . that [is] the challenge to Bolshevik [Communist] propaganda.[7]

Her resolve never wavered, even as famine swept across northern China in the region of Kiahsien in 1921. With the famine came sickness and poverty, leaving orphaned children to fend for themselves. After Sun's death in 1925, confusion reigned as Chiang Kai-shek took over party control. The fighting against powerful warlords in the central plains continued for years. The worst situation existed in Honan. In the years 1926–27, the Communist wing of the government incited riots among the laborers and peasants. Farmers and radical laborers joined with the bandits, adding to the chaos. Many of the severely injured, who were bleeding and dirty, were brought to the mission dispensaries on makeshift beds. Missions and missionaries withstood increased disorder amid the fighting. However, news from the mission fields worsened as bandits wreaked havoc on the workers.

> We have been disturbed by robber bands for many years. It was risky to travel far from railroads. Other cities were captured by big bandit bands. Then missionaries were often carried away and held for ransom. Rev. Lundeen and Mr. Forsberg were carried away by such robbers once and kept for several months. Rev. Vikner was also held a few days and then liberated.

—Rev. Alfred Trues, missionary, Honan, China[8]

The antireligion movement grew rapidly during the years of unrest. The church faced increased opposition, the destruction of property, and violence at the hands of soldiers and Chinese bandits who added to the fray. Mission buildings were often occupied by troops. The mission workers continued their work, but not without fear and concern for their safety.

> It became clear the soldiers were not the ordinary Chinese army but trained by Russian communists and skilled Chinese militants. Their plan was to overthrow the warlords in the north. . . . As the nationalists pursued their course, it became evident that they were not friends of the missionaries . . . [and] a reign of terror followed in their wake.

—Rev. Victor Swenson, missionary, Honan, China[9]

Missionaries found it more difficult to distinguish between the bandits and the soldiers, the latter of whom may have provided some protection. The Red Guard or Red Spears, a group of young students trained in Russia as revolutionaries, frightened everyone. They had a dark side, often ransacking homes and intimidating villagers, touting the teachings of Chairman Mao. Opposed to old ideas, cultures, and customs, they indiscriminately destroyed symbols that they determined were feudal, capitalist, and radical, such as Christian schools who taught about Jesus.

One evening I had the whole group of fifty schoolgirls rush in with their faces pale as could be and so scared they could not utter a word. The Red Spears were looking for robbers outside the compound. They were shooting and causing a great commotion. The girls spent the night sitting as packed as could be on the floor of my study where they felt safe.

—Ethel Aikens, school principal, Honan, China[10]

The missionaries had reason to worry about their personal safety. Due to the arduous travel upriver, the bandit district existed beyond the reach of law and order. Hordes of soldiers and robbers roamed the countryside, with tales of bandits raiding and carrying off captives and "committing excesses upon them" regardless of class or nationality.[11] The bandits considered missionaries to be radical "dogs" who represented imperialistic Western values. As such, they were attacked, often with brute force. Once, during Sunday worship services, they confronted the parishioners.

Suddenly there was a noise at the entrance of the compound and in rushed a body of men with red spears. Fortunately, they stopped at the entrance of the chapel. The sermon was continued, but with what feelings need not be mentioned.

—Rev. Herman A. Larson, missionary, Honan, China[12]

The missionaries remained optimistic despite the difficulties, the hostility, and a government in shambles. In fact, Rev. John Leonard Benson wrote to the WMS suggesting Emmy, at age sixty-nine, visit China despite the dangers. "Let me assure you that we shall all most gladly welcome you to China in the future and shall be praying that nothing may hinder you from paying us a visit," said Benson.[13] The request went to a vote, and in August 1926, the WMS Executive Board agreed Emmy should go as a representative to the triennial meeting of the General Assembly of the Lutheran Church in China. Emmy sent two cables, one to accept the invitation and the other to inquire as to the safety of such an undertaking.[14] The trip, fraught with peril, would take Emmy nine months to complete.

To pay for her journey, each member of the WMS donated one penny. Additional money came from the WMS field fund, and another one hundred dollars from the *Mission Tidings* profits. Although there was no guarantee of secure travel, Emmy found the prospect of visiting the far-off missions along the King's Highway thrilling. "King" referred to Jesus Christ. The highway was not actually a road, but the name given by the WMS to the string of mission posts across China, India, Africa, and the Holy Land. The "road" consisted of sixty-three buildings built by the WMS. "Wherever the footsteps of Christian women pass on the King's Highway, you may see hospitals, orphanages, Bible schools, and other schools, and homes for strangers, springing up similar to daisies on a path," said Emmy. "The King's Highway not only encircles the earth, but it is the world's longest and most beautiful road of safety."[15] For women and children, the "road" was a place to go for health care, an education, and a refuge from the war.

Emmy's adventure began in September 1926. For her, the trip to Asia and the Middle East represented a lifelong dream. She would gain firsthand knowledge of the WMS mission posts and journey to Jerusalem. Happy for the opportunity, she visited a beautiful alabaster mosque in Cairo and held ancient biblical scrolls in Samaria.

Upon her arrival in China, the army soldiers, intrigued with the elderly women, set aside half a boxcar for Emmy and her friend Mrs. Landstrom. The soldiers occupied the other half as the train journeyed sixty miles through the countryside.[16] The armored boxcars, shielded with metal plates, had small square windows. During the trip, the soldiers shot at the insurgents on the ground, who fired back.

No seats and no heat in the boxcar made the trek uncomfortable. Emmy slept from dusk to dawn on the floor with one thin blanket underneath her and another blanket pulled up over her to escape the cold.[17] "We were forced to travel in coal cars and ammunitions cars that in this country would be abandoned as freight cars no longer fit for duty. There were no stations and the only way that we were able to get a ride at all required permission from some high officer in the army," reported Emmy.[18]

Mule carts—two-wheeled wagons hitched to a mule with an awning over the top to protect travelers from the sun—provided local transportation. This mode of travel offered a wee bit more comfort than the train. Nonetheless, the bumpy ride tossed passengers from side to side as the pack animals navigated unpaved roads.

The journey allowed Emmy to see the mission fields for herself, including the groundbreaking ceremony for a new hospital in Hsucháng (now Xuchang), China. Due to the war, the district had been evacuated, but the conflict did not stop Emmy. The festivities were held at midnight in the pouring rain. Emmy's shoes sank deeply in the mud, covering the tops of her shoelaces. All the while, fighting arose a mere five miles away.[19]

She also visited the Emmy Evald girls' school in Hsuchow, founded in 1922. (The institution went coed in 1939 and named the Pei Deh Middle School.) Emmy relished her trip to the mission school where she met her "little jewels," as she called them. Hearing them sing carols on Christmas Day as they lit candles erased any travel difficulties from her mind. "These young people will be our hope, our joy, our pride, our crowning victory," said Emmy.[20]

The two-story building, which sat on approximately 8.5 Chinese acres, cost $20,000. A brick wall surrounded the property for safety. Simple furnishings, including chairs, small tables, and a wooden blackboard, filled the classroom. The Chinese did not use stoves; hence the unheated room caused frozen hands and feet. But the biggest threat to the students and the staff, aside from the Red Guard, was scarlet fever, which could be highly contagious.

The girls followed an orderly regimen and a curriculum akin to those found in American schools. The morning began at five thirty, which gave the girls a chance to dress before attending to their studies between six and seven in the morning. A breakfast of millet, porridge, and bread arrived at seven thirty. Other meals consisted primarily of rice, vegetables, and sweet potato, with little meat. Students took part in devotions three times during the day along with afternoon study periods. The girls had four hours of religion, catechism, Bible history, and Bible study every week.[21]

* * * *

Communications to America were sporadic. When nobody had heard from Emmy during her China visit, alarm rose. Had she been captured by bandits or even murdered? Emmy's daughter Lillian wrote to the newspaper, resulting in the following *Chicago Tribune* article appearing in the January 19, 1927, issue:

Seeks News of Mother

Uneasiness concerning the whereabouts of her mother, Mrs. Emmy Evald, Chicago missionary, yesterday brought a telephone inquiry to The Tribune from Mrs. Lillian Carlson, 1453 Berwyn Avenue. Mrs. Evald, who is prominent in the work of the Augustana Lutheran Church of America, left San Francisco in September for a world cruise with Mrs. J. W. Landstrom of 1030 North Central Avenue.

They have been for some time in the interior of China and visited many of the Lutheran Missions. At Hsuchow, China, they were to attend the dedication of the Emmy Evald High School building. . . . Nothing has been heard from them for nearly two weeks. . . .

Emmy and her companion were safe from harm. Their disappearance resulted from a breakdown in communication, and the Chinese Christians prayed that "Grandma" Evald would return to the United States safely.[22]

It is with no small sense of loss we bid them [Emmy and Mrs. Landstrom] goodbye. We have learned to appreciate their unfailing optimism in the face of constant dangers from wars and banditry and the many inconveniences to which they have been exposed. In these days of stress and turmoil, we needed just such encouragement to spur us on and keep us from losing heart.

—Rev. Benson[23]

Emmy did need to defend herself on one occasion, however. With more than a dozen reels of film tucked away in her carpetbags, she sat on the dock while waiting for a boat when a Chinese man, thinking her bags were filled with money, tried to steal them. At nearly seventy years of age, Emmy beat his hands with her tight little fists until he dropped her bags. He ran off surprised and ashamed that he had been struck by a woman—and an elderly one at that!

* * * *

Next on Emmy's agenda was an excursion to India. Upon her arrival, six hundred women from ninety-six different villages marched distances varying from ten to twelve miles to hang garlands about her neck in gratitude.[24] She made many friends in India, such as Raja, a Lutheran bishop, and his wife, Ruby. The families remained friends for generations.

The snake, however, was another matter. While sleeping in a tent at one of the mission field stations, Emmy awoke to see a venomous viper with its keeled scales, triangular-shaped head, and elliptical eyes snuggled in her cot. She lay motionless for an entire day until the snake abandoned her bed. Thinking of her family, she prayed as her muscles strained to remain and her stomach growled with hunger, not daring to move. God had other plans for her, which did not include a poisonous ending.

During her travels, she sent postcards to her grandchildren, telling them of her trip and reminding them of different Bible stories, such as Joseph and his coat and Jesus's teaching in Galilee. She found one postcard of an Egyptian sphinx especially beautiful and instructed her granddaughter to save it. Eighty years later the postcard was found among her granddaughter's papers. Emmy's word was gospel.

Emmy returned to the United States in June 1927, excited to be home again. She and her companion told of the killing, looting, and abuse in China. According to Emmy, her experiences were far less treacherous than those of the missionaries who lived there. Emmy's trip reinforced her belief in mission programs, and she emerged an even stronger advocate for the work being done.[25]

Emmy brought souvenirs for her family to enjoy. There was holy water from the River Jordan, which her two youngest granddaughters used to baptize neighborhood children in their backyard, charging each child a nickel. No doubt Emmy was unaware of the scam or punishments would have been handed out.

Emmy also purchased dolls from different countries for the girls. Every Christmas, she made doll clothes for them. Once when the home caught fire, the firemen, attempting to extinguish the flames, did more damage with their axes than the actual fire. The dolls were lost but never forgotten.

Other souvenir items included three Oriental rugs, a carved teak elephant, and a teak table. The table legs were shaped as elephant heads with genuine ivory tusks and long trunks. Some of the grandchildren favored a Chinese puzzle box that they took to school as a show-and-tell item.

* * * *

Most missionaries and other outsiders fled China in 1927. Many boarded Chinese junks and prepared to leave when the military government warned them of the danger. For Protestant China, it was the worst scenario in its history. Anti-Christian attitudes were widespread and persecution frequent. Personal property was destroyed, leaving the missionaries and their families uncertain as to their future.

> It is nearly impossible to keep soldiers from occupying our property. Books, dishes, furniture, and household goods are stolen or destroyed. Our chapels are used for stables by the soldiers.

> —Rev. Swenson[26]

In February 1928, Rev. Benson wrote of the dire need for emergency expenses for the evacuation of mission staff from China.[27] Sixty missionaries exited the country at a tremendous cost to the WMS. While the dollar amount of property damage could not be tallied, the WMS presumed their losses to be heavy.

* * * *

Meanwhile, Emmy was embroiled in a firestorm of a different kind. Augustana College and Theological Seminary, an institution cofounded by her father, had since moved from Paxton to Rock Island, Illinois. The location was chosen because of its proximity to the railway that connected it to Chicago and westward. Emmy called the move a mistake. "Father could have purchased the entire block of Chicago and Dearborn for $5,000, now worth millions and millions, instead of moving the college out to the countryside in Rock Island," she had said.[28]

Her reflections were incorrect, however. Her father and his associates never considered Chicago as the permanent home for the college. Today the liberal arts school, which is the oldest Swedish American educational institution in the country, remains in Rock Island and sits along the Mississippi River amid the rolling bluffs of Rock Island and Moline, Illinois, and Davenport and Bettendorf, Iowa. Although the college began admitting women in 1870, they could not earn degrees until 1885. (Emmy received an honorary master of arts degree from the college in May 1922.)

Student life changed at the college after World War I. The influenza epidemic and the rising cost of living had impacted their finances. Only two new buildings had been built in the previous twenty-five years, and the gym maintained an unpaid debt of $75,000.[29] The Ladies Hall, originally a home built in 1876, converted into a women's dormitory in 1888. Now filled to twice its capacity, the hall was deemed too old and unacceptable. Forty women shared two bathrooms, one of which lacked a sink, forcing some residents to kneel over the bathtub to brush their teeth from the faucets. Others slept in the attic. Some rooms contained three cots and served as a passageway to the next room, offering little privacy. The hallways were dark, and the unpainted floors made for splinters on bare feet.[30]

"It is astonishing how many insist on calling it 'Ladies Hall,' now that it is entirely out of date. Let us be up to times and call it the 'Woman's Building.' All of us can agree not to call it [the] Woman's Dormitory," said Emmy.[31]

She felt the college had a responsibility to see that the women were adequately housed. After all, the students had come from good Lutheran families, who expected that their college training would compare favorably with other educational institutions. The need for a new ladies' dorm was urgent, if only to safeguard the girls' welfare.[32] Initially, the college sought funds from local businesses in and around Rock Island and Moline without significant success. Therefore, the college turned to the WMS to come up with the cash for the dormitory, and an overwhelming majority of women accepted the challenge after a daylong discussion.

On Wednesday morning, September 21, 1921, fundraising for the Woman's Building began, aided by Emmy's son-in-law Rev. Hoffsten and members of the WMS. Dr Andreen, the college president, opened the meeting with a rousing speech. Soon after Emmy took the floor and fireworks set off. "The women of the synod have made no mistake in placing her upon the committed in charge, as she is a most forceful and eloquent speaker," printed *The Augustana Observer*.[33]

Emmy, who was outspoken and accustomed to getting her way, was strategic in her fundraising efforts. Focusing on women's rights and equality, she published a brochure in English and Swedish illustrating young women standing outside the gates of the college with suitcases in hand. The caption read, "Shall we close Augustana's gates and bid our daughters to go elsewhere for lack of suitable living quarters?"[34]

The WMS set a goal of $150,000. WMS members sponsored "dormitory teas" in every congregation within the synod to fortify the building fund. The estimated cost of furnishing a dorm room for two women was $175. Only the finest construction of mahogany or walnut was deemed acceptable. Donations were gratefully accepted and thought to be an extension of the WMS's overall missionary efforts, that is, providing suitable housing for female students preparing for work in the mission fields.[35]

Having accumulated $120,000, the women of the WMS felt entitled to voice their opinion regarding the location and plans for the dorm.[36] (Some references stipulated the WMS donated $121,000; another claimed they donated $109,658 of the $200,000 needed for the new dorm.)[37] To stimulate interest in the project, Emmy hired an architect, Olof Cervin, to select a suitable site—

perhaps a bit prematurely. She was about to lock horns with the college.

The architect's drawings for a modern residence hall, which incorporated new ideas from large universities, was presented to the WMS Board of Directors.[38] After such an effort, Emmy had hoped to have definite plans and specifications for the dorm. However, no final plans could be adopted while the building site remained undetermined.

The WMS proposed a building at the corner of Thirty-Eighth Street and Eighth Avenue, currently part of the new theater building. Due to its higher elevation, the location lent a certain air of prestige since it was above the marshy areas that covered most of the campus grounds. However, the theological faculty objected because the new site would block their view.[39] An alternate site down the hill on the north side of Seventh Avenue was proposed by the college's architects, Perkins, Fellows & Hamilton. At one point, Augustana's president, Dr. Gustav Andreen, saw some merit in the WMS plans, to which Mr. Fellows responded, "I think Mrs. Evald has you hypnotized."[40]

Emmy objected to the alternate building site because it was too "close to the car barns and too near the athletic field,"[41] and she did not want the women crossing a busy street to attend classes. In a quandary, Augustana's board members elected a committee to meet with the WMS. In May 1923, the board recommended the Seventh Avenue site once again. In protest, Emmy threatened to return the money to the original donors, resulting in a bitter fight.[42]

Emmy called for more prayer regarding the building location and wrote to the property owner, George Johnson, concerning the availability of his property priced at $15,000 with $1,000 to be donated by him.[43] Dissension existed within the WMS as well. A group of women from Rock Island, disturbed because decisions were being made in Chicago, sided against Emmy, and gathered 375 signatures from those who endorsed the college's alternate building site.[44]

Discussions carried on between the college and the WMS. Would Emmy win? That was the question everyone wanted to know. On February 1926, Augustana's all-male board proceeded with its architectural plans and built the women's dorm on Seventh Street, at which time Emmy and the WMS refused to relinquish the funds.[45]

Subsequently, during the synod's convention, the men asserted their power over the woman's society for the first time in years and directed the WMS to transfer the money to Augustana. In April 1927, the money was given to the college, although it fell short of the $200,000 building costs. Not surprisingly, the women turned down the board's request to put up the additional money to cover the deficit.[46]

Several months after the clash, the directors of the college acknowledged the misunderstanding with the WMS concerning the construction of the women's building. Mrs. Andreen, wife of the college president, commented, "Those who had worked hard to push it [the Eighth Street location] through were made to feel like those of unsavory reputations who were not wanted and could scarcely be tolerated."[47]

The new dorm was dedicated in August 1927, but tensions continued to run high, and nobody from the WMS attended the ceremony. After its completion, 135 women stepped into their new home. At a loss as to what to call the dormitory, the college simply called it the Woman's Building, or "WB," as it was affectionately known by the women who lived there.

Oddly enough, the WB would become the site of the first recorded panty raid in February 1949, when two to three hundred men, aided by a few female students who opened the doors, stormed the hallways for ten minutes. Surely the incident would have shocked Emmy and the WMS whose upbringing stemmed from the Victorian Era. The WB remained the oldest residence hall for women until 1960, when the building was converted to a men's dorm and was renamed the Erland Carlsson Hall after Emmy's father.

Emmy's legacy continued for years. The men's lounge was dedicated in her honor in March 1999. When the building was refurbished in 2008 to house academic offices, it was renamed the Emmy Carlsson Evald Hall for the woman who had fought so hard for its existence, perhaps righting a decades-old wrong.[48] It is one of four buildings on campus named for a woman and serves as a reminder of her accomplishments. The structure is now a centerpiece of the college campus with landmark status. If the WMS had won the fight, the building may have been torn down to make way for new construction.

* * * *

Battle-worn, Emmy continued her travels around the United States, giving illustrated lectures on China and India. "Every time a new building has been needed in some part of the world . . . Mrs. Evald has started out on a speaking tour," wrote Anabel Parker McCann of the *New York Sun.* "This speaking invariably made the fifty-cent pieces drop faster into the society's treasury. It is said that few clergymen in the Lutheran Church are more popular or powerful 'persuaders' than Mrs. Evald."[49]

But before she took off for another tour, friends and family celebrated her seventieth birthday at the Stevens Hotel. Located on South Michigan Avenue in Chicago, the hotel was one of the grandest hotels in the world at the time of its opening in 1927. (The Stevens Hotel is now the Hilton Chicago and remains one of the poshest hotels in the city, known for its exquisite lobby and ballrooms.)

The cost of the luncheon was two dollars a plate. Attendees dined on sweet melon cups, chicken breasts with a delicate mushroom sauce, vegetables, and crisp salad greens. For dessert, all who attended relished a rich strawberry parfait and petit fours.[50]

Women from different Lutheran synods attended the birthday bash along with Methodists, Baptists, and other mission friends. Most of the women were from Chicago; others arrived from across the country. Representatives from ten different organizations in which Emmy had been involved also shared in the festivities. Numerous letters and telegrams arrived from well-wishers around the globe. McCulloch gave an address. Addams, her college roommate and founder of Hull House in Chicago, was unable to make the party but sent birthday greetings and a small gift.[51]

* * * *

A local Worchester, Massachusetts, newspaper referred to Emmy as "one of the most prominent, most influential, and most widely known Swedish-American women in the country." The paper went on to say, "She is a forceful speaker, and, as an organizer and executive, she has but few equals among Swedes in the United States."

Emmy's dedication to mission work and devotion to the church made an indelible mark on the women she led. But not all was well. Emmy had her share of critics, some of whom were clergy. Not all men accepted the role of women within the church, especially a forceful one determined to have her way. Some decided a woman's influence was dangerous . . . a "wicked experiment."[52] Although women had won the right to vote, they were still expected to "know their station." As church ladies, the religious community expected them to adhere to the traditional Christian values of compassion and submission. In their view, the WMS had clearly overstepped its bounds.[53] Although Emmy's vision was clear and her determination abundant, her fight with Augustana College and Theological Seminary signaled the beginning of the end of her reign as WMS president. It was the close of an era and the start of a new decade.

Chapter Seven

Life at Berwyn Avenue (1930–1940)

After World War I, Chicago experienced a booming economy. Without sophisticated media, people relied heavily on what they could observe, and their lives saw little change. People continued to purchase goods and large-ticket items, such as automobiles and appliances. In rural agricultural areas, the outlook was completely different. Warning signs abounded, including foreclosures, falling crop prices, and the selling of livestock. The 1930s would be a roller coaster: a decade marked by comings and goings, highs, and lows. For Emmy, good times mixed with the bad, and triumph accompanied defeat.

But for now, life went on as usual. The Swedes sought more affordable housing and moved outside the city limits to neighborhoods such as Andersonville, located on Chicago's North Side in the Edgewater community. Andersonville, once a cherry orchard, was easily accessible via the "L." Within its boundaries locally owned businesses thrived along with doctors and dentists. Aromas from Nelson's Bakery permeated the air. The Linn Brothers Funeral Home offered their services for $125. Knight's Grocery & Market provided fresh fruits and vegetables, and Holgersen Brothers Hardware supplied an assortment of items for the family home.

Emmy, too, left the city proper and purchased a three-story frame house at 1453 Berwyn Avenue in the heart of Andersonville near Clark Street. The Craftsman-style home had six bedrooms and featured a front porch and a swing for cooling off on hot summer evenings.

The bedrooms filled up quickly as a collection of family members came to share Emmy's home. The Carlson family was first to arrive at the Berwyn Avenue address, having moved from a nearby rental home on Balmoral Avenue. The crowd included daughter Lillian, son-in-law Amel, and their children. Reynold Erland was the eldest child. Burley Richard was second oldest. Emmy's two granddaughters, Emmy Charlotte and Jean Gertrude, completed the household along with the family dog, who was not allowed upstairs.

Emmy loved flowers and fresh vegetables, especially asparagus, and planted a small garden in the backyard. The alley behind the house provided a haven for the grandchildren to play ball or ride their bicycles away from busy streets.

Inside the home Oriental rugs covered the hardwood floors. Emmy's baby grand piano sat in the corner of the living room. Two of her oil paintings hung on the wall. A built-in hutch, filled with Limoges china, occupied an entire wall in the dining room. The opposite wall displayed an ornate mirror above the buffet. Burgundy drapes adorned the sunlit windows. The dining room table sat twelve, providing ample room for guests.

Emmy's bedroom was on the second floor. Shoeboxes, with their contents clearly labeled, rested on closet shelves. Her black lace dress hung in the closet for special occasions, and a black seal coat kept her warm during Chicago's cold winters.[1]

Preferring the quiet hours after the family had retired for the night, she often worked into the wee hours, seldom retiring before one or two in the morning. Ensconced in her third-floor study with papers piled like flapjacks on a plate, she spent eleven to fourteen hours a day writing her column for the *Mission Tidings* newsletter and scanning the WMS financial statements. The *Lutheran Companion* magazine once stated that "the WMS and its many departments were so complex only Mrs. Evald understood them, so God let her run it [the organization]."[2]

Emmy was fond of saving newspaper clippings, which included everything from local news events to household hints. Scores of articles on women's fashions, recipes, and poetry filled the cabinet in her office. On occasion, she would ask her grandchildren to dust and straighten the books in the bookcases, paying them a small reward.

The home was filled with love and laughter. Lillian delighted in entertaining as the children sat quietly on the stairs watching and listening with their noses peeking out from behind the railing. Leftover desserts were eagerly devoured by the foursome the following day. Lillian and Amel were also members of the Swedish Club in Andersonville and active in the Sunbeams and the Moonbeams, adult fellowship groups, at Immanuel Lutheran Church. Grandson Rey babysat his younger siblings when his parents went out for an evening. He was known to jump off the stairs, grab hold of the chandelier, and swing himself into the hallway, scattering shrieking children into the living room.

Emmy traveled a great deal, but once she returned home, she always had time for excursions with her grandchildren. Picnics, pony rides, and ice cream cones were standard fare at the Lincoln Park Zoo. The family went to the circus when it was in town and took their lunch to Riverview Park, billed as the "world's largest" amusement park. Fastened tightly in their seats, you could hear the grandchildren's screams as they rode the Bobs, a wooden roller coaster with an eighty-five-foot drop. Emmy watched as they went around on the seventy-horse carousel. The last stop was the little train. "*Mormor* [Swedish for grandmother] was asking so many questions of the engineer that we thought she was thinking of buying one [a little train] for us. One day we walked over to the stables on Clark Street to see where the ponies went to sleep at night," said Ruth, another of Emmy's granddaughters.[3]

Christmas Eve was a special time when the extended family gathered. Warm, buttery scents of ginger and nutmeg filled the kitchen as the women made Spritz butter cookies pressed into different shapes, such as stars, camels, and wreaths, and thin ginger cookies known as *pepparkaka*.

Emmy took time away from the kitchen to set up a train under the tree, which, with all the small parts, proved to be a time-consuming project that kept the small children busy for hours. Meanwhile, *dopp I grytan*, or "dippa greason," as the grandchildren called it, cooked on the stove. Family members dunked hunks of bread into the large pot of steaming beef broth and ladled chunks of meat and vegetables into a bowl while other holiday preparations were being made.

A traditional Swedish smorgasbord was served for Christmas dinner, including *lutfisk*—a salted fish served in a cream sauce—blood sausage, and *Änglamat*, a dessert made with heavy whipped cream, lingonberry jam, and *skorpor*, akin to biscotti. The dessert was so light and airy, the younger children named it "angel food." (*Änglamat* is also Swedish for angel's food.)

"Once the table was cleared and the dishes done, Emmy pulled out dolls, games, and paint sets with stencils to bring out the children's artistic talents," said Ruth.[4] An artist herself, Emmy hoped one of them would also develop the talent. Swedish folklore dictated that *Tomte*, the Christmas elf, arrived that evening. But before the gifts were distributed, the grandchildren gathered around the piano, perhaps not too enthusiastically, and sang "Brighten the Corner Where You Are" and the Swedish folk song, "Children of the Heavenly Father," two of Emmy's favorite hymns.[5] The household woke early on Christmas day to welcome the Christ child. The *Julotta* service at Immanuel Lutheran Church began at four o'clock in the morning. (*Jul* means "Christmas" in Swedish and *otta* "before dawn.")

There were house rules to be followed. Emmy was a stern disciplinarian. The Sabbath was strictly observed. The Carlson children were expected to sit quietly with folded hands or read the Bible on Sundays. In the summer, the family occasionally drove north to Bangs Lake after church. During the trek, the children read aloud from the Bible and Emmy gave a sermon. Reciting Bible verses with the windows rolled down was especially embarrassing at stoplights.

When the children misbehaved, they sat on dining room chairs, lined up like pencils against the wall, as punishment. When their father, Amel, came home from work, he squeezed their hands, releasing them from their imprisonment. Granddaughter Emmy once spent an entire day at the dining room table peering down at a cold, gelatinous bowl of oatmeal, which she had refused to eat at breakfast.

But most days at the Berwyn home were ordinary. Emmy kept busy with the WMS, and the children went off to school, while their father, a vice president for the Checker Cab company, headed for work. Nobody was prepared for the financial crisis that would send the country into a tailspin.

Behind the mask of the city's prosperity lurked unregulated banks. At the time, folks did not understand how banks operated in terms of leveraging assets and borrowing. On October 29, 1929, when the stock market crashed, the country was taken unawares. The slide into the Great Depression was a long one, lasting well into the thirties. Unemployment gripped large industrial and manufacturing areas. As banks closed, panic seized the nation. Large crowds of able-bodied men lined the streets, unable to obtain work. In Chicago, homelessness reached epic proportions with "hobo" camps constructed of cardboard and scrap wood springing up under Lower Michigan Avenue and in Grant and Lincoln Parks. Squatters lived in empty railroad cars and dug for food in trash cans. Gangsters turned to violent crimes.

Emmy turned off the heat in part of the house to save money. After school, the grandchildren ran into the warm kitchen, where an afternoon snack awaited. A stockbroker who lived across the street hanged himself in the basement, and several church members killed themselves. Emmy's granddaughter lost her life savings—all twelve dollars—at the local bank.

* * * *

The winter of 1930 was unseasonably mild. Temperatures pushed toward forty degrees in February—still one of the mildest Februarys on record. But spring would have to wait. When March winds blew at thirty-five miles per hour, Mother Nature dumped a record-breaking nineteen inches of snow on the city, with drifts up to five feet clogging the streets and making travel hazardous.

Death came uninvited to Berwyn Avenue that year. Grandson Burley, with his red hair and angelic face, had a heart condition. A simple medical procedure could have repaired his heart, but medical technology had not progressed that far. At age twelve, Burley awoke in the middle of the night on December 6. With one last breath he screamed, "Sweet Jesus, help me."

As was the custom, he was laid out in the living room. His grieving father sat at the kitchen table all night and wept. His remaining siblings stayed in the shadows frightened at the sight of their brother's corpse lying motionless. Emmy, who was out of town at the time, came home and met her daughter on the front steps of the Berwyn Avenue home, where they hugged and cried together. The funeral at Immanuel Lutheran church ended with one final hymn, "Going Home," adapted from Dvorak's Symphony No. 9. Burley was buried in his Boy Scout uniform and laid to rest in the family plot in Graceland Cemetery in Chicago. He was the second grandchild lost to Emmy. Gertrude Hoffsten, an adorable cherub, had died on October 8, 1918, at age two.

Death came knocking once again in 1932, when her brother Eben passed away. Emmy flew from New York City to Lindsborg, Kansas, for the funeral. The plane ride was a first for Emmy at age seventy-five. With airplane travel being so new, there were delays. Lillian, understandably so, was concerned for her mother's safety.

Additional changes occurred when Sam, Emmy's remaining brother, now widowed, moved into the Berwyn home after his retirement from a sales position. When he could not sleep, he played one of his two violins. His melodic notes floated through the house as family members slumbered. On several occasions, Sam's daughters, Ethel Rabbit and Edith Gustafson, came to visit him, adding to the household. Granddaughter Ruth also lived with the family for two years and worked as Emmy's secretary at the WMS headquarters on Pine Grove Avenue.

Now in her mid-seventies, Emmy experienced some hearing loss and depended on her family members to be her ears. She also used a hearing aid housed in a black box the size of a pencil box, which weighed about seven pounds. Although it was portable, the long cord connecting the box to the earpiece was cumbersome. When newer models came to market, she bought one.

"I went along on errands and I really had to walk fast to keep up with her. Batteries for her hearing aid were a must on her 'to do' list. It was a special joy when the batteries were so tiny that she could pin the hearing aid under her blouse and put the earpiece directly into the ear," said Ruth.[6] Although Emmy was not a vain woman, a less conspicuous hearing aid was a bonus.

* * * *

The economy finally began to turn around when President Franklin Roosevelt created the Works Progress Administration in 1935, renamed the Works Projects Administration (WPA) in 1939. The program meant new jobs for millions of out-of-work laborers, allowing American families to crawl out from under the Great Depression.

Word of a second world's fair in Chicago brought renewed hope. In honor of the city's centennial in 1933, Chicago hosted the "Century of Progress." The fair, which originally ran from May to November 1933, was located along Lake Michigan between Twelfth and Thirteenth Streets on the Near South Side. (The site is now home to McCormick Place and Northerly Island Park, formally Meigs Field.)

Consistent with the dazzling white Columbus Exposition in 1893, this fair was conceived during a financial crisis. But in contrast, planners opted for a rainbow of colors to depict the 1933 expo. Their choice, designed to bolster consumer confidence in the US economy, projected optimism and opportunity. Bright lights symbolized a better tomorrow. Women did not have a role in the planning, however, nor did the fair include their contributions to society.[7]

Coinciding with the fair was the first-ever All-Star baseball game between the American and National Leagues. The July 6 game, held at the former Comiskey Park, home of the Chicago White Sox, featured Lou Gehrig and Babe Ruth in the lineup. The American League won four to two. The game, known as the Midsummer Classic, is still played.

The following summer was aptly named the "dust bowl" summer. Temperatures reached into the nineties in May 1934. The family on Berwyn Avenue endured clouds of dirt from the plains of Kansas and Oklahoma that rained down on the city as thick as face powder, engulfing it with an estimated twelve million tons of grit. High winds drove dust and grit into every crack and cranny of their home. Drifts of ash piled besides buildings as the black blizzard hung in the air for five hours before blowing eastward toward Philadelphia and New York City.

Despite the heat and the grime, the world's fair reopened from May to October 1934. Emmy's family were among the many visitors, which averaged around one hundred thousand people per day. Dubbed the "Journey to the Future," exhibits included the modern home with a dishwasher and air conditioner, "dream" cars, and other new modes of transportation, such as the Zephyr streamlined train.[8] More than one husband was chastised for watching Sally Rand, a burlesque star, and her famous fan dance.

By mid-July, a scorching heat wave spread over the city so intense that the record has not been broken for more than eighty-five years. With less than one-half inch of rain in the month, the city and its residents were parched. The Carlson children watched as the grass turned wheat colored; leaves on the trees curled with thirst and dropped to the ground. Emmy's garden withered, and the earth cracked. The temperatures were cooler by the lake, but nobody noticed. Not long after, the citizens read that public enemy number one, the notorious gangster John Dillinger, was shot and killed outside the Biograph Theater.

On Memorial Day that year, the family laid wreathes on Erland's and Carl's gravesites (Emmy's father and late husband, respectively). Her granddaughters, Emmy and Jean, were confirmed at Immanuel Lutheran Church and attended their first confirmation class reunion, a tradition started by Emmy in 1903.[9] As the year ended, grandson Rey enrolled in a master's economics program at Northwestern University in Evanston, Illinois, while his sisters attended Senn High School on Chicago's North Side.

* * * *

In 1935, Rockford College selected Emmy to be its representative at the commencement exercises of Upsala College in New Jersey, which had Swedish roots and a Lutheran connection. As a Rockford alum, Emmy's devotion to education and her inspirational leadership among women made her an obvious choice.[10] Plus she was nearby in New York City on WMS business.

Emmy, who received an honorary degree, beamed with pride as she marched down the sidewalk with sixty-two other graduates. Wearing her doctor's cap with a gold tassel and black robe with velvet trim, she was as enthusiastic as a young schoolgirl. Her presence delighted those in attendance. The campus, inspiring in its beauty, added to the glorious day.

"In the early afternoon, the academic procession began. In that procession marched a great, little woman," wrote Associate Professor Joshua O. Lindstrom. "Many friends were assembled on the spacious lawn. If any one incident could be thought of as being the climax to an unusually fine commencement at Upsala College, it was the conferring of the Honorary Degree of L.H.D., Doctor of Humane Letters, on Mrs. Emmy Evald."[11]

The degree, with all its "rights and privileges," was bestowed upon her on June 3, 1935. As Lindstrom presented the degree, he said, "To the most outstanding woman of Swedish descent who, because of a great service, may it also be said merits a place in that noble band of the Lord's ministering women."[12]

Newspaper accounts reported that "the university's president doffed his cap and draped a hood of blue and gray around her shoulders that had borne the heavy burdens of an exacting WMS office. She was handed a bouquet of flowers and the simple rite was over," said Bengtson.[13] (Several other notable citizens have since been honored by the liberal arts college, including Dag Hammarskjold, a Swedish diplomat and secretary general to the United Nations, and the poet Carl Sandburg, before its bankruptcy in June 1995.)

Friends gathered on the lawn to extend their congratulatory wishes. Speeches were given, prayers said, and hymns sung. The spectacular day came to a lovely end, symbolizing the appreciation felt by Upsala College and the Augustana Lutheran Synod.

Rockford College honored Emmy once again by choosing her to represent it at the inauguration ceremony of Upsala's new president, Dr. Evald Lawson.

Dear Dr. Lawson:

Indeed, we should feel highly honored to have Dr. Emmy Evald represent Rockford College at the inauguration service of the President of Upsala College. Dr. Evald is one of our most distinguished alumnae and one of whom we are exceedingly proud.

—Dr. Mary Ashby Cheek, President, Rockford College[14]

Although she was young at heart, Emmy was probably the oldest representative to attend the ceremony. Because Dr. Lawson was named after her late husband, Carl Evald, she was thrilled to witness his installation.

"I have never seen a president's inauguration and it was perfectly grand with seventy-five colleges and universities represented. As Rockford College was started in 1847, I was in the eighth row in the procession and it swelled me with pride to honor the college that I attended," said Emmy.[15]

Her happiness was short-lived, however, when troubles surfaced at Berwyn Avenue. Her daughter Lillian's marriage was coming apart. The crash of '29 had complicated their married life. Amel worked several odd jobs, but money was scarce, and Lillian's grief after Burley's death was unending. Emmy, who received a widow's pension of fifty dollars a month, faced additional problems of her own as her relationship with the WMS deteriorated and newsletter subscriptions dropped to a new low with a loss of more than 1,400 readers.

Making matters more difficult, P. O. Bersell, president of the Augustana Synod, restructured the home mission boards, uniting the male and female boards whereby the men and women were to work jointly. However, because the synod was predominately male, they controlled the decision-making process, putting the WMS under male authority once again. Whether the actions were meant to stifle the women or were economic in nature, the outcome was just the same . . . devastating.

The women offered a compromise and asked for membership on the board of home missions. But all the funding was to pass through the men. To lose control over their treasury was a terrible blow to the WMS, especially to Emmy, who was not known to share the reins of leadership. For the first time since its inception, the WMS was in turmoil. Their mission work continued, but the lackluster reports were equivalent to air leaking from a balloon.[16] (By 1942, women were represented on all the major mission boards, but they were in the minority and could achieve little, if any, influence. Cooperation between the men and women did improve, however.)

* * * *

As the years passed, more accolades were in store for Emmy. In recognition of her years of service, the trustees at Rockford College for Women announced that a section of the new $150,000 library, soon to be built, would be named Emmy Carlsson Evald.[17] A second alcove honored her classmate Jane Addams.

"It would be a great inspiration to our students to be reminded of the splendid contribution which you [Emmy Evald] as an alumna of the college have made to the life of the Lutheran Church and to the country at large," said Cheek.[18]

Funding for the project ($25,000) grew thanks to the efforts of her college chum, who wrote letters to Emmy's friends and acquaintances outlining her many accomplishments. "This memorial for a living woman will please her and will hold future Rockford College students to a high standard of Christian virtues, womanly graces and civic loyalties," wrote McCulloch.[19]

The alcove, located in the fine arts room of the John Hall Sherratt Library, contained many books of Scandinavian literature, art, and culture, and was dedicated on October 20, 1940.[20] Emmy was happy to be honored by her alma mater and recounted her fond memories.

> It is indeed a great honor to me that the trustees will give to Emmy Carlsson Evald a section in the new library. (I worked in the library the years I was at Rockford College.) It is a strange coincidence that I have the honor to be remembered along with a section named for Jane Addams as she and I roomed side by side in Linden Hall.

> —Emmy Evald[21]

Members of the Lutheran synod also rejoiced with the news "of this well-merited distinction for one of the noblest daughters of the church and one of America's most outstanding citizens."[22] (In July 1960, work began on a new campus. In March 1968, the old campus was demolished, including the library.)

As the decade closed, the invasion of Poland by Nazi Germany loomed, hinting at the war to come. Emmy continued to champion women's issues, but this time in New York City.

Chapter Eight

The Lutheran Home for Women (1930–1935)

During the 1930s, Americans looked to the government for relief and to generate jobs that would kick-start the economy. The WPA created new jobs in Chicago, including a downtown construction project to expand Lake Shore Drive, one of the first high-speed, limited-access highways. In 1934, the Federal Deposit Insurance Corporation was created to further protect bank account holders. Additional regulations were also placed on commercial banks. But millions of men and women around the country remained unemployed.

With several banks closing, some of which held WMS assets, various chapters worked to make their pledges. Their existence appeared as fragile as eggshells.

> Dear Mrs. Evald,
>
> . . . The Home Mission pledge is a little short this year, but that is because of the low price of eggs. When eggs come back to a good price, we have no fear of meeting our pledge. I think we have done well in the face of hard times. Eight banks failed in the Wahoo District, yet they gave the biggest sum to mission since they have been a society. . . .
>
> Much love to you,
> Elna Johanson, Omaha, Nebraska[1]

Despite the financial turmoil, the WMS continued its mission efforts. "Hold fast" committees were formed to hold on to the gains already achieved.[2] In time, work began assisting migrant workers in California, including Mexicans in Los Angeles and African Americans in Oakland, as these needs and opportunities presented themselves.

Appeals were made for Asians living in Vancouver, British Columbia. The monies raised allowed the WMS to purchase a two-story structure with a wraparound porch at the corner of Tenth Avenue and Cypress Street. The building became a "tiding over" home for girls, many of whom were the descendants of Chinese immigrants hired in the 1880s to build the Canadian Pacific Railway. The house was small but comfortable.[3]

The need for a similar home in New York City had often been discussed. Shortly after the Vancouver purchase in 1929, the WMS membership approved such an undertaking. New York City was an entry point for immigrants coming through Ellis Island and a mecca for unskilled labor. At the time, it was reveling in an era of prosperity and growth, including the construction of the Chrysler Building and the Empire State Building in 1930 and 1931. The expanded mass transit system made it possible for women to get work as nannies or domestics in the high-rent district along Park Avenue.[4]

However, the city had its darker side. There were rent riots in the Bronx and strikes in Harlem. The unemployed sold apples on the street corners for a nickel. Children played a made-up game called "Eviction," or "Going on the Dole," imitating the world in which they lived.[5] These were desperate times for some. Young girls often disappeared from city streets and were sold into white slavery (known as sex trafficking today).

Undeterred, the WMS began to raise money toward the purchase of a building in the Big Apple comparable to the one in Vancouver. They asked church members for donations, including young people who were expected to give two dollars each.[6] The WMS selected Emmy to head the search committee and charged her with the task of finding a suitable location for female immigrants.

Emmy's business sense in the world of high finance enabled her to take on building operations, such as the New York City facility. But money was tight, and the WMS could ill afford to relax its penny pinching.

Upon her arrival, she met with other committee members: Dr. and Mrs. J. Alfred Anderson, Mrs. Henry Miller, and Miss Signe Stolpe. Together they set out to secure a site for the girls' home with the aid of a realtor from a large real estate firm. As luck would have it, they found a settlement house on their first day, which was owned by the Jewish Sisterhood of Service.

The red-brick property at 318–320 East Eighty-Second Street was fireproof with two immense doors at the entrance and a portico to protect visitors from the elements. The generous interior comprised two large rooms on each of the five floors, a roof garden overlooking the city, two top-notch elevators, and a large gym in the English basement, which was a half story above ground. Although the price was thought to be reasonable, at $100,000, the cost was much too expensive for the WMS.

The committee sought to uncover an alternative. They considered tearing down a cluster of older houses to make room for a new building. But the cost, which might have run upward of $500,000, was considered prohibitive. An exhaustive search continued for nearly a month without any progress. Now weary and discouraged, the committee disbanded and went their separate ways.

Before returning to Chicago, Emmy obtained the blueprints of the settlement house and asked the architect Cervin, who had helped her with plans for the women's dorm at Augustana College, to assess the possibility of remodeling the building. After much reconfiguring, he designed a plan, which illustrated a newly renovated settlement house well suited to the committee's needs.

Meanwhile, the real estate firm in New York City informed Emmy that a group of doctors had offered $85,000 for the settlement house and suggested the WMS outbid them by $1,000, if they were still interested. Instead, the women decided to offer $80,000 in cash.[7] But where would they get the money?

After a lively discussion at the annual convention in Rock Island, Illinois, the women agreed to use $50,000 from the China hospital fund, which could not be used due to the civil unrest in that country.[8] All but the Minnesota delegation voted their approval.

"Ignore the Minnesota delegation and do not show them that you care," wrote Johanson. "It is a shame to let them spoil nearly every convention." She was convinced that the Minnesota delegates were out to "nag" Emmy.[9]

With most delegates in agreement, the remaining $30,000 was financed at 5.5 percent interest through the Emigrant Industrial Bank of New York to be repaid over the next eleven years.[10] With money in hand, the Jewish sisters accepted the WMS's offer on June 2, 1930. The honorary president of the Jewish Sisterhood explained that God told her to sell the building to the WMS because they were working on behalf of others.[11]

Emmy, who was graced with a keen business sense, recognized the building was an exceptional buy and praised God.

> One must be a New Yorker to appreciate this big bargain and a real estate person with a vision. The elevator alone is worth $8,000 to $10,000. We felt God wanted us to have it. After sixteen strenuous days of real estate hunts, we found nothing cheaper, nothing better. May God bless this new undertaking.
>
> —Emmy Evald[12]

The sale came as a shock to the cynical New York City realtor. "What a surprise. This is the first time in all my life that I have heard that almighty God had anything to do with New York real estate," said the realtor.[13] The transaction was probably the first and last time God ever intervened in the purchase of such a property.

The deal, completed in October 1930, was a miracle indeed. The land alone, which equaled two lots fifty by one hundred feet, was estimated to be worth at least $80,000. In addition, the Jewish Sisterhood donated furniture, office equipment, a kitchen range, and a secondhand hot water and steam boiler valued at $1,500.[14] And the location was good for what the WMS could afford. Centered in the heart of Manhattan, the dwelling was within walking distance of Central Park, several bus lines, and the subway station at Eighty-Sixth Street, in addition to popular shops and churches.[15]

The society's excitement came to a screeching halt, however. Earlier that year, city leaders had passed a new ordinance that disallowed any remodeling to the building. What could they do? At a loss, Emmy sat with an acquaintance, Mrs. Olson, in the vacant building, their voices echoing in the empty halls. Unsure of their next step, they invited the search committee to the building lobby for coffee and prayer to discuss the future.

Another miracle unfolded when Emmy and Mrs. Olson went to Gimbel's department store. While shopping, they bumped into Mr. Ferris from the Missouri Lutheran Synod. He, too, had difficulties with the city and recommended Mr. Stern, a "little, bright Jew,"[16] to assist them. They met with Mr. Stern, who agreed to help, but the days lingered into months.

Many anxious prayers winged their way toward heaven, asking for God's helping hand in the situation. Thanksgiving passed, and autumn faded into winter. Christmas came and went, and still there was no word from Mr. Stern—or from God, for that matter.[17] The five-story building sat empty and virtually worthless.

Emmy characteristically relied heavily on her faith and trusted others to do the same. "We are living in a day of testing. The world is aching with fear, crime, and strife, and men and women are forgetting God entirely,"[18] she wrote. "Puffs of wind in our days make it easier for us to lose our faith in God. Hold fast."[19] Despite Emmy's encouraging words, the unknown weighed heavily on WMS members.

After anxious months, a building permit arrived on January 15, 1931, with a stamp of approval for the architect's plans, much to the committee's relief.[20] After four months of waiting, there was cause for rejoicing. At last, friendless and homeless girls in New York City would have a safe home in which to stay.

Emmy participated in construction projects, often studying blueprints and overseeing the building process brick by brick. The Lutheran Home was no exception. Emmy spent much of her time in New York City during the renovation supervising the work. In fact, she lived at the home during the demolition amid dust and flying plaster and the pounding of sledgehammers.

One wintery morning, a search committee member found Emmy bundled in a sweater and boots on the fifth floor of the home. She was directing the workmen, who towered over her in size and strength. "She even carried one door frame herself and placed it where she thought it should be," said Stolpe.[21] The workmen were equally amazed at Emmy's participation.

Construction was one task facing Emmy, furnishing the building was another. With the renovations near completion, the WMS needed money to refurbish the rooms. Financial appeals went out via Emmy's column, Among Ourselves, in the *Mission Tidings* newsletter. "Dare you do nothing?" she wrote in response to the white slavery happening all too often in New York City. "Dare you give nothing? Dare you stand in the way of those who willingly work to rescue the poor girls?"[22]

The plans called for a large sunlit living room, a sewing room, an office, and a big reception hall. Each of the sixty-five bedrooms would be light and airy, and each floor would have a laundry. All total, there would be eighty-two rooms, sixty-nine closets, and eight bathrooms to equip. The job was a huge undertaking, but Emmy was not worried. Instead, she encouraged every district to donate $200 toward home furnishings.[23]

She also suggested selling bricks to help with donations. Bricks could be "purchased" for ten cents apiece and could be sold to anyone—man, woman, or child—regardless of their religious affiliation. Young women and junior societies were expected to help with sales as well. Emmy reminded prospective donors that those who gave early in effect gave twice because the money could be used that much sooner.[24]

Her message rang out to different districts, many of which offered to "adopt" a room in honor or in memory of a member. Once the rooms were habitable, the WMS began its search for a resident supervisor to oversee the home's operations.

Their search began at the Deaconess Institute in Omaha, a boarding school for the education and training of young women to become deaconesses. After completing their training, the students were sent forth to do charity work. Sister Veda Johnson was from the institute and thought to be the perfect candidate. But she was young and lacked experience for such a formidable job. Dr. Emil Chinlund, director of the institute, voiced his concerns. Nonetheless, Sister Veda was hired at $600 per year plus room and board. She also received one month's vacation, travel expenses to and from Omaha, and in the case of illness, up to one month's sick pay.[25] Everything appeared to be settled, or was it?

Under her management, household accounts evaporated like rain on a hot August afternoon. Clearly, she was not up to the task. The WMS board took swift action and voted unanimously to send her packing.

Sister Veda was shocked at her recall. Dr. Chinlund wrote to the WMS suggesting her dismissal would be an embarrassment to the Lutheran Home and requested additional information regarding her recall. After all, her appointment had been made urgently and over protest. He also asked if she might at least have a hearing or serve as an assistant to Emmy, who, as WMS president, oversaw the home's operations. His request was denied.[26]

Things went from bad to worse when Emmy was stricken with a severe illness in May 1934. At the annual WMS conference in Rock Island, Illinois, she refused to accept the nomination for president despite receiving the most votes and many encouraging remarks. Peterson took over as WMS president. Emmy's explanation for her actions was related to stress and not her age, as some might have expected.

> No, I did not refuse to be reelected as the WMS president because of my high age. It was for other reasons. I do not realize that I will be seventy-eight years of age in September, full of vigor, health, and strength—in God's wonderful gifts. The last four years have been the most strenuous years of my life. I am not the worse for it, though I wish it had been more harmonious and congenial with some members of the Chicago board.[27]

Although Emmy indicated a desire to turn the reins over to other capable hands, she was the leading spirit of the organization, and letting go after forty-three years at the helm was difficult. (Emmy was named WMS president emerita in 1935.) Rev. Conrad O. Bengtson, pastor of Immanuel Lutheran Church in Chicago, stated that the events at Rock Island were mingled with sadness and regret.[28]

After her resignation, Emmy hoped the executive board would see fit to keep her busy. Instead, they offered her a pension, and a resolution to that effect was adopted immediately. But Emmy's work was her joie de vivre. She asked for a job in lieu of retirement. Without further ado, the board asked her to continue her work at the Lutheran Home by becoming its resident manager. The "LH," as it was affectionately called, would be the last jewel in Emmy's crown, her grand finale. She was also to remain as a WMS representative on the board of foreign missions until the hospital in China was completed.

Emmy said goodbye to Chicago and embarked for New York City with her daughter Lillian and two granddaughters, Emmy and Jean, in 1935. On the way to the city, they stopped to visit Emmy's nephew Egbert and his family.

> Our folks entertained quite a bit, and although my brother and I did not realize it at the time, our most famous guest was Emmy Evald. She was traveling from the Midwest to New York City with her daughter and granddaughters in the early 1930s.
>
> She was a striking woman, although rather short and squarely built. She wore a long black dress with a choker collar and carried (what seemed huge) a black box—a hearing aid. She was very kind and attentive to my brother and me. She took a twenty-minute nap after lunch, as was her custom.
>
> —Lars E. Carlsson, Emmy's grandnephew[29]

The boys never forgot the occasion. Although they were young, Emmy's visit etched a lasting impression, as she did on most people.

While the women headed for New York City, Emmy's grandson Rey and son-in-law Amel, now separated from Lillian, stayed in Chicago. Emmy rented out the Berwyn Avenue home to her neighbors, the Anderson boys, who bought it for $10,000.

* * * *

The layout of the LH was perfect for large gatherings. The vestibule was furnished with benches, a table for notes, and a bronze plaque, honoring donors. The reception hall was ten feet wide and forty feet long with a runner of Oriental design. A side table and gilded mirror sat in the hallway with slipper chairs on either side. Landscape paintings decorated the beige walls.

Emmy's bedroom suite was on the main floor just left of the front door. The room was furnished simply with a desk, lamp, and dresser. Her jewelry, including earrings and a watch pin, were artfully arranged on top of the dresser along with pictures of her late husband and other family members.

Her bed was three-fourths in size, which was larger than a twin but smaller than a full-size bed. Although she could have requested otherwise, she always made her own bed. She did not wear makeup. "Painted" faces were reserved for the theatre and social climbers. But her medicine cabinet did contain skin lotions and special "potions" for her face, leaving her skin with a sweet smell of lavender and rosewater.

Emmy's office, which was in the adjoining room, was filled with file cabinets, a desk, two chairs, and a telephone. Stacks of papers adorned every available surface in her "little nook"—on window ledges, her desk, and the bookshelves. The switchboard, designed for incoming calls, sat behind her desk with a chart showing the occupants of each guest room. As Emmy's daughter and assistant, Lillian occupied the bedroom and office next to her mother's.

The elevator was down the hall. Its heavy walnut doors opened to a second cagelike metal door which clanged as it opened and closed. The elevator was large enough to accommodate six people comfortably, but only Emmy had the keys to unlock its doors.

The living room's four windows overlooked a grassy area. The fire escape and a public phone were located on the left behind the baby grand piano. A large painting of Emmy hung over the fireplace. Three couches and easy chairs were grouped along the windows to facilitate conversation. In the center of the room was a carved rectangular table for magazines. The setting was well appointed and inviting.

Upstairs, each floor had a communal bath with four sinks, four stalls, and one bathtub, plus a sewing room at the end of the hall. Each simple room contained a metal bed frame and mattress, table and lamp, and dresser with a big mirror. Every room had a window and an area rug.

During the summer months, the roof garden provided the only green space to be enjoyed for blocks. A Ping-Pong table, an old upright piano, and chairs were available for the residents. Emmy's grandson Rey donated shrubs for the planter boxes, which accented the space. Although Emmy seldom had time to enjoy fresh air and sunshine, she loved watching the sparrows, who made frequent use of the small birdbath.

Residents also had access to laundry facilities as well as snacks found in the huge refrigerator in the kitchen. The storage room, which measured forty by seventy feet, was in the English basement. Nobody was allowed there without Emmy's permission. Trunks and larger pieces of luggage could be stored in the "trunk" room for an additional charge of fifty cents per month.

* * * *

The LH was considered the next best thing over the Young Women's Christian Association (YWCA) for those who were self-sufficient, temporarily unemployed, or without means. For immigrants needing an affordable room, it was perfect. Rates were reasonable. Rooms rented for two dollars a night, including breakfast. Dinners were eighty cents during the week and one dollar on Sundays and holidays. Permanent residents paid eleven dollars per week for a double room and twelve to fourteen dollars for a single, which included two meals a day. After six months, women were given three weeks of reduced rates. Feeling quite safe, nobody locked their doors.[30]

Businesswomen and students of moderate means could stay for five consecutive years. Others were accepted on a transient basis. References from a pastor and a business acquaintance were required of all permanent guests and were subject to Emmy's approval. The girls cooperated with the established rules. No typing was allowed after nine in the evening, and radios had to be turned off by ten thirty. If a guest endangered the health and happiness of the other guests, the home's board of directors had the authority to remove her.

The home averaged around forty girls a month. Emmy held firm that every resident must pay for room and board, making it clear that the LH could not operate as a charity. However, she did "carry" some of the girls who were without work for short and sometimes longer periods of time. At one point, the residents were asked to donate two dollars per head toward reducing the debt on the property due to the WMS Executive Board's concerns regarding the mortgage. Overall, the German, French, and English residents were happy to pay. But Swedes from less affluent families were less willing.[31]

The LH was no small household. In one year, 743 women stayed a night or up to a year, plus eight missionaries on their way to or from the mission fields, and several pastors and their families who were visiting New York City.[32]

As resident manager, part of Emmy's job was to publicize the home as a haven for young women and provide the residents with spiritual care. In addition to overseeing the home's everyday operations, she was to produce monthly reports for the WMS Executive Board and solicit financial support for the home.[33] Although Emmy never learned to drive, she had no problem getting around the city. She would take public transportation or her daughter, who owned a green Ford, would chauffeur her.

Her transition into the job, however, was anything but smooth; storm clouds began to gather. She was no ordinary employee and did not expect to be treated as such. After all, as the founder and former president of WMS, she felt entitled to a certain amount of respect. But when the subject of her salary arose, things got off to a rocky start. Should her pay be taken out of the WMS general operating budget, as was done with Sister Veda's salary, or should it be a paid out of the proceeds from the LH? The issue grew into a war of words between Emmy and the WMS Executive Board in Chicago, putting her at odds with the board.[34]

In contrast to the dissonance with the WMS, the staff at the LH adored Emmy. She helped wherever she was needed, putting up jams and jellies in the kitchen, applying her know-how elsewhere, and inspiring others with her keen sense of humor and dedication.

The laundress had one of the biggest jobs at the LH. All the bed linens and towels were provided by the home. Mattresses were turned weekly for even wear. Two cooks prepared the meals. A buffet breakfast of eggs, cereal, coffee, tea, and bread was served from seven thirty to nine in the morning. The fire alarm, which was not connected to the fire station, signaled the dinner meal at six in the evening. Before dinner, the women gathered around the baby grand piano to sing "What a Friend We Have in Jesus."

The dining room sat sixty-five guests, who ate at long tables with white linen tablecloths and napkins. The meal was standard fare but nourishing. Mealtimes for the family varied. Emmy ate breakfast by herself at a round table at nine in the morning after the crowd departed. After her meal, she often discussed the week's menu with the head cook. Lunch was prepared midday for Emmy and Lillian. Her granddaughters could eat in or grab a bite at Ronny's Delicatessen, famous for its ice cream sodas. In true Swedish tradition, coffee and sweets were available in the afternoon for Emmy, Lillian, and Emmy's secretary, Ellen Holt. For special occasions, the family went to the Gothenburg Restaurant for a smorgasbord or Schrafft's on West Fifty-Seventh Street.

A smorgasbord of *lutfisk*, turkey, herring, and headcheese was served at Christmas dinner at the LH. Friends and family gathered for the holiday festivities, bringing good cheer to those who might otherwise be lonely. After the meal, a special program began in the living room, which was decorated with evergreen garlands, candles, a Christmas tree, and a crèche. Carols were sung, and small gifts were distributed to everybody in attendance. Even a fifteen-cent box of stationery or a tiny book of poems was warmly received. For many residents, who lived far from their families, it would be the only gift they received.[35]

Compared to the residents, Emmy's usual attire, a black ankle-length skirt, long overblouse and jacket, and her signature choker necklace, might have suggested another era.

Guests at the LH ran the gamut. Occasionally, Emmy entertained friends or family, such as Catt, suffragist and leader of the League of Women Voters. When Catt came to visit in the summer, she stayed in the Bridal Suite, so called because it was ivory in color.

Other guests included missionaries from Africa and China, whom Emmy helped to resettle in the United States.

Residents included couples such as Stanley and Stina Peterson, who lived in one of the first-floor guest bedrooms. Mona Stopenbrink, who worked at the Lenox Hospital, started using drugs and was presumably evicted. Orphans Ingrid and Solveig Inglasrud from Norway stayed for free. One tenant worked as a Swedish masseuse and another worked for the Diamond Match Company in Mount Kisco, New York. There was a German girl named Karen who played her accordion for the members of the German American Bund, a pro-Nazi political organization. One night she headed out the door for work and never returned, leaving her belongings behind.

Perhaps one of the most unusual characters was Julia Bergen with her gleaming red hair. As a lady's maid, she had traveled all over the world with her mistress but never stepped out of the stateroom. When the top button of her dress fell off, she fastened it with a red and blue pencil. She was quite a sight with newspapers stuffed into her stockings, presumably for warmth.

Julia was responsible for answering the phone and earned a dollar an evening as the night doorkeeper. She sat by the door from seven to eleven at night. Short in stature, she stood on a stepstool to peek out the tall window at whomever was knocking. After eleven o'clock, the door was locked, and a key was required to gain entrance. Emmy's teenage granddaughters were known to steal a key from Emmy's office to let themselves in after a late-night party—risky business had they been caught.

Despite Emmy's watchful eye, other shenanigans transpired at the LH. Her granddaughter concocted a scheme with another resident, Grenhult Strope. Strope worked as a nanny and a cook on Park Avenue. Whenever she started a new assignment, Emmy's granddaughter Emmy, who worked part-time in the office, sent a telegram wishing Strope a happy birthday. Following the telegram, the new employer bought her employee a gift to celebrate the occasion. The ploy worked every time, much to the delight of the two women.

The same granddaughter wrote a class assignment about the women at the LH.

It was my fortune or misfortune, I have never quite decided which, to live among the girls at the Lutheran Home for two years. The Home, as we called it, could better be explained as a residence club for women in the style of the YWCA.

"The girls" was a favorite expression used by my grandmother when speaking of her large family. Such a conglomeration of people you would not believe. They varied from Chinese missionaries to wrapping girls in Macy's. Somehow, they seemed to represent a wandering tribe of detached folk without homes or ties of a home. Every few years they shifted from one residence club to another. Being misfits in normal life, they found their happiness with the Home, a haven for lost souls.

Among the older and more permanent girls were the retired old dears. Retired from what was always a moot question. They boasted of rich husbands, though some of them did manage a paltry living off their dead husband's insurance. Stories of the "gay nineties" stacked higher and higher until they would fall and need rebuilding. Some of the old dears turned to religion as a last thought of this earth. These fanatics would contrast beautifully with the "ex-gay nineties" and worldly lot.

The middle group of the girls was made up largely of domestics. Never had I considered the home life of maids and where they might choose to live. Of course, they had to live somewhere; I might have guessed the Home. Most of these domestic girls were of Scandinavian birth and had come to America to work for better wages. Once they saved enough money, they waited expectantly for a boat returning to Sweden or Norway.

For those that stayed longer there was a chance of becoming a part of a great estate or retiring at the Home for time eternal. As a group these people never seemed sure of their direction. The whole scheme seemed a futile one.

The girls in the literal meaning of the word were still another group. They were young and eager but gave up easily. Most probably each one had come to the big city with big ideas on how to stir the world or crash Broadway with a bit part if possible. They were a stage-struck lot and spent endless hours at the stage entrance of Broadway theaters, hoping in their own dream world, for an audition. After an approximate six months' time, all was considered lost, and Father's last check saw them safely home again.[36]

In truth, employment opportunities for young women were changing. A decade earlier, immigrants who arrived in New York City did what they knew best. They worked as live-in help in private homes taking care of the house, washing, ironing, and cleaning. They answered the door, accepted packages, and took phone messages. The jobs did not pay much, but it was often more than what they could earn back in the "old country." Wages ranged from $30 to $55 per month, which by today's dollars was about $400 to $720. Cooks could earn a bit more.[37]

During the 1930s, however, housewives enjoyed more conveniences, such as electric washers and dryers, vacuum cleaners, and electric mixers, easing their day-to-day chores. The need for live-in servants declined. Household help continued to be the main employment option for women, but other jobs, such as office help, salesclerks, and factory workers, now opened to them.[38] In addition, some of the LH residents studied at the Julliard School, Columbia University, or the Katherine Gibbs secretarial school.

"Living out" provided young working girls a room of their own with more privacy and more freedom.[39] Plus, there was a sense of camaraderie among the guests, many of whom were from Sweden or Norway and spoke a common native language. The women also had a place to stay on their days off. In their free time, they could shop, stop for a soft drink, or attend church.

On Saturday morning, September 18, 1937, Emmy celebrated her eightieth birthday. The day began early with lighted candles and red roses as Emmy's daughter tiptoed into her room singing first in Swedish and afterward in English. At the breakfast table, beautifully adorned with more flowers and candles, the residents at the Lutheran Home sang a rousing chorus of "Happy Birthday" as Emmy entered the room. She remained amazingly spry and equally busy, attributing much of her strength to her college friend Jane Addams who was equally active within the realm of social work.[40]

Nearly four hundred cables, letters, and cards came from well-wishers around the world, and enough flowers to fill an entire room in appreciation of all her good works. Some sent gifts. A special congratulatory message and words of praise came from the WMS Executive Board, thanking her for her energetic efforts and sending a bouquet of love consisting of eighty roses.

More than two hundred guests attended her birthday party, organized by Emmy's closest friends, and enjoyed cake and coffee. The gathering sang yet another round of "Happy Birthday" and Emmy's favorite hymn, "What a Friend We Have in Jesus." Prayers and testimonials filled the afternoon, bestowing upon her the title, "Mother of Missions."[41]

Appreciative, Emmy published a kind note of thanks in the *Mission Tidings* newsletter to all who attended her milestone celebration, attributing her good health to God. "By grace he made me a little tool in my Master's hand. I will always praise and thank the Lord for this great privilege," said Emmy, who was quick to acknowledge God's blessings in her long life.[42]

Following the festivities, Emmy, laden with birthday bouquets, took the train to Chicago to visit her brother, Samuel, who had fallen seriously ill. She gave some of her flowers to her brother and laid the remainder on the graves of her parents and husband at Graceland Cemetery.[43] After a lengthy hospital stay, Sam, Emmy's one remaining sibling, passed away in October 1937 from complications associated with diabetes.

* * * *

Over time, the home showed a profit due to Emmy's efficiencies. Sister Veda's habit of ordering groceries over the phone may have caused her to overspend. Emmy, on the other hand, walked to the Second Street farmers market. Leonard, the handyman, who was in his mid-thirties and knew little English, accompanied her with a large cart for carrying home the vegetables and desserts. All who knew her at the market gave her a special price. Turkeys, roasts, and chickens were purchased elsewhere.

At one point, Emmy went back to Chicago for a visit. Upon her return, she fired the staff and hired different employees through the Brooklyn and Gustavus Adolphus Lutheran Churches, which presumably helped to make the home more solvent. However, the action could have been out of her loyalty to the church members.

As the years went by, Emmy served as a "mother" to more than fourteen thousand guests, guiding and advising them during their stay. Nearly one-third of the residents were from Sweden. Others came from twenty-nine different countries and thirty-four states.[44] "It was like a party," said Emmy's granddaughter in her later years.

* * * *

The Emmy Evald Auxiliary, which consisted mostly of ministers' wives, was the backbone of the home. The group of one hundred members held their monthly meetings at the Gustavus Adolphus Church, located at 150th and East 22nd Streets. Its main jobs were to increase donations and handle publicity for the home. The members also proved to be a source of strength for Emmy during more challenging times.

"I am grateful to God that he made me go to New York. He rewarded me and gave me such loyal and helpful friends as I have had in the Emmy Evald Auxiliary. . . . We could not have continued our mission if [it] had not been for them," said Emmy,[45] who was ever thankful for the auxiliary's aid and support.

Most of the members of the auxiliary resided in New York, but some lived as far away as California. To keep everybody informed, the auxiliary began publishing a newsletter, *Glimpses*. Annual subscriptions were twenty-five cents. Readers were asked to share news and current events from their locale.[46]

Fundraising efforts continued for the purchase of new bed linens to replace worn ones and to pay down the mortgage. Concerned over the safety of the banks, Emmy recommended any accounts in Merchants Bank be withdrawn and put in a bank vault at a cost of three dollars.

"If you do not follow my advice and it goes wrong, it is not my fault, because I have warned you. If you really understand the nature of this scare, each one must keep quiet . . . as the bank authorities might come back on us and prosecute us," wrote Evald to the WMS Executive Board.[47] After the stock market crash, many folks were leery of banks. Whether the WMS heeded her words of advice is not known.

While the LH appeared to be flourishing, events on the Pacific Coast were quite different. The Vancouver home continued to falter due, in part, to high unemployment and the end of migration. Sadly, the home was also in need of repairs, redecorating, and new plumbing. Despite several changes in matronship, the number of guests declined. Unable to pay the bills and bothered with persistent matron issues, the WMS Executive Board searched for the right leadership. Finally, under the supervision of Julia Finden, the home started to see a financial turnaround.[48] Nonetheless, the WMS turned the Vancouver home over to the board of American missions in 1942.

Meanwhile, the discontent brewing between Emmy and the WMS Executive Board in Chicago was about to come to a full boil.

Chapter Nine
The Showdown (1935–1938)

Basic accounting principles and procedures were at the crux of the disagreements—and, perhaps, stubborn pride. Emmy and the WMS Executive Board had differing opinions regarding the decisions made at the 1934 annual convention in Rock Island, Illinois. Several issues were up for debate. How should the income from the home be used, and who was accountable? How should matters be handled now that Emmy had resigned as president? What began as minor skirmishes between the board and Emmy heated up with missives fired back and forth between Chicago and New York City.

Some blamed the WMS board members for the misunderstandings; others blamed Emmy. Both accused the other side of mistakes in the annual reports, citing that accounts were incorrect and that the official minutes of the Rock Island convention did not accurately reflect the actual events of the convention.

Questions arose. How should the home's mortgage, held by the Emigrant Industrial Bank in New York, be paid? The WMS finance committee felt that, after expenses were paid, any proceeds or profits from the home's rental income should be sent to them in Chicago. The committee, in turn, would make the mortgage payments. Emmy argued that the mortgage should be paid from the WMS's general operating budget and not the home's profits. Furthermore, her lawyers believed that profits from the home could not be mailed out of state.

The finance committee responded that surplus monies could not be considered profit because the LH was in debt to the Emigrant Industrial Bank. Surely debts could be paid outside the state of New York, they claimed. The committee also requested a copy of the legal statute in question. The matter was finally resolved in favor of the finance committee, requiring mortgage payments be paid from the home's receipts.

Also in dispute were donations for new bed linens and home furnishings. Were these bills remodeling expenses or equipment purchases? The New York auditors stated that, if the former were true, the WMS treasurer should pay the estimated $4,500 out of the WMS's general operating budget.[1] The executive board disagreed.

Relationships disintegrated further when Emmy learned her salary of one hundred dollars per month would be paid from the home's receipts rather than the WMS's general operating budget. She viewed the action as a breach of contract and a request for her resignation.[2]

"What does the board mean by breaking my contract . . . when I was called to rescue the home? If my salary is stopped, will it mean that I shall leave the home?" asked Emmy.[3]

She had endured many hardships, but this was the worst heartache to come her way. Her lifelong friends whom she had worked with for decades now turned against her, or so she thought. "It is the greatest insult that could be hurled at one who has saved the situation of the home and worked for mission causes for forty-three years as the WMS president. It is like putting a dagger into my heart from an ungrateful board," wrote Emmy.[4]

Equally alarmed, the directors of the LH sent a protest letter to WMS president Peterson, exclaiming that they, too, were shocked by the action. They also considered the board's decision a breach of contract and insisted that Emmy remain in the home until the matter could be resolved.[5]

The executive board intended no harm. Theirs was a business decision. Did it really matter which fund was used to pay Emmy's salary? In their opinion, now that the home was well established, expenses, such as salaries, should be paid from the home's receipts. They were astonished by the accusations, claiming they had no plans to fire Emmy. Nonetheless, the board insisted her salary be paid from the home's receipts.[6]

Other disagreements arose regarding payment for Emmy's daughter and grandchildren, who helped in the kitchen one summer when the LH was shorthanded.[7] The executive board wondered why her family was paid for the entire month of June when they had not arrived in New York City until June 20. The LH directors replied that the check, issued in July, covered their employment from June 21 to July 21. In addition, they admonished the executive board for questioning the payment without first investigating the facts.

"You should have checked . . . before drawing conclusions," wrote Mrs. Alfred Anderson, vice president of the LH directors.[8] She went on to say that family members had helped busing tables, painting the roof garden, and assisting with the laundry, among other chores.

The arguments waged on. To stay current, the WMS Executive Board wanted to adopt new ideas and business methods. But Emmy saw no reason to alter the way in which things were handled. She submitted financial information to the board as always, but they were not fully itemized as the board wished. The board sent Emmy frequent letters requesting more documentation. Emmy, on the other hand, concluded a change in reporting could not be done without the approval of the home's directors, who would not meet again for several months.[9]

The board was direct and firm in its response. "Send them at once," was the reply. "The executive board is entitled to know every detail of every department within the society and must know to function properly. Please cooperate in this matter."[10]

Tempers flared. In September 1935, Emmy wrote to the WMS Executive Board to explain that scheduling conflicts and out-of-town travel prevented her from sending the summer financial statements and reminded the board that they had never been delivered before September.

"There has never been any complaint in the past three years, why should there be any now?" she wrote.[11] The executive board responded, "We did not look upon your financial reports as being overdue. We are looking for January's reports, which have never been received."[12]

They were at a stalemate. Emmy's many achievements preceded her. Was she trying to hold on to one last shred of control? Was the board being disrespectful? Feelings on both sides were hurt, with no resolution in sight.

With so many financial issues in dispute, Emmy asked for a new accountant, claiming the audit committee was one-sided. The board was satisfied with the current accountant. Emmy argued the recent "dustup" was meant to hurt and humiliate her, and signed her letter, "your lonely and sad friend."[13] Board members were offended by Emmy's remarks but arranged for a new auditor just the same.

The situation deteriorated even more when Miss Highland, the *Mission Tidings* editor in chief, refused to print Emmy's column, Among Ourselves, in the newsletter. Furthermore, Emmy was to submit her articles to the editor. Emmy complained that she had founded the newsletter and had written her column for decades. Angered and dismayed, she refused to write another word.[14] They are "false friends," one mission worker alleged in Emmy's defense.[15]

To clarify the issue, the WMS Executive Board explained that the new WMS president would write the Among Ourselves column under her own byline. To avoid repetition, everybody was to submit articles to the editor, including the new president. Given Emmy's valued experiences and information, they hoped she would continue to contribute news articles.

For a while, it seems as if she and the board were on friendlier terms. But when news of a building project for the LH, which included a new kitchen and expanded trunk room for greater storage, reached the executive board, it was the last straw. Emmy had authorized the work even though the board had tabled the project for further review. The question arose as to whether the relationship could continue.[16]

At the March 1938 WMS Executive Board meeting, it was reported that "Dr. Evald was so impossible neither they nor the board of directors in New York City could do anything with her."[17] In addition, the board claimed Emmy was uncooperative in all matters relating to the home. They also determined that at age eighty, Emmy was too old for such a responsibility. The vote was near unanimous (twenty-six to five) that she be retired with a $600 pension and a new matron hired, effective July 1, 1938.[18] The board notified Emmy of its decision in a letter and expected her to vacate the premises.

When the board of directors in New York heard of the decision, they wrote their objections, saying they knew nothing of the accusations made against Emmy. In addition, every member of the Emmy Evald Auxiliary, New York district pastors, and the LH residents petitioned the board in Emmy's defense. Hundreds more wrote protest letters, but all were ignored.[19]

However, at the forty-seventh WMS annual convention, which was held in New York City on June 22, just days before the deadline, attendees took no action regarding Emmy's future. Instead, they deferred the subject of her retirement to the WMS Executive Board members, who were attending the convention.[20]

There was a lot at stake. Even with a pension, Emmy would have no place to go. Her daughter Lillian, who worked as Emmy's assistant director, would be unemployed at age fifty-two, and Emmy's two teenage granddaughters would be on the streets of New York, literally.

The board's first step was to retain New York attorney R. C. MacFall to review its legal rights pursuant to the home. He advised them not to meet with the LH directors at the home as it might ignite a firestorm. Instead, he would communicate with Albert Schatz, Emmy's attorney, to learn if Emmy were still there. Indeed, she was.[21] She had disregarded the board's letter.

The situation was as messy as a teenager's bedroom. Could a solution be found? Thoughts of selling the home were considered. But the idea was deemed too impractical and one that might split the WMS into two camps: for and against Emmy's removal.

In reviewing the facts, MacFall concluded that the executive board had the authority to oust Emmy. But because of some confusion regarding the home's bylaws, he warned the board that a case could be argued against them. Emmy's attorney stated that she was responsible only to the home's directors in New York and not the WMS Executive Board.[22]

Clearly the situation called for a diplomatic solution. MacFall cautioned board members that by submitting Emmy to this kind of humiliation, they might jeopardize the good works of the organization. While he recognized they had the legal right to remove her, and that they had tried to retire her gracefully, he hoped the board would come up with another solution.[23]

Tensions rose to an all-time high when the WMS Executive Board sent a telegram to Emmy requesting a meeting. Emmy, the LH directors, the auditors, and Schatz were asked to meet with the WMS board members in McFall's office at eight in the morning on July 1 to discuss Emmy's removal from the home.

When the day arrived, Emmy and her entourage gathered around a large table in the lawyer's office, quietly discussing the merits of the WMS Executive Board's accusations. As they waited, some checked their watches for the time; others sought the restroom. The clock ticked, and the minutes passed, but there was no sign of the board members.

It was now nine o'clock and still no WMS board members. After waiting an hour, the group began to stir, stretching in their chairs, tapping their feet, and drumming their fingers impatiently on the table. Some watched out the window for a sign of the executive board women, while others squirmed in their chairs awaiting the showdown.

Finally, at ten in the morning, a telegram arrived. The executive board members would not be coming. Instead, they had decided to take the train back to Chicago.[24] Emmy had won. The board had backed down, allowing her to stay at the LH.

Epilogue

Emmy remained at the LH as its managing director for years to come and made a lasting impression on the women of her generation and beyond due to her faithful service and zeal for mission.[1]

In honor of Emmy's eighty-fifth birthday, the Emmy Evald Auxiliary threw a huge party at the LH. Two hundred guests attended the auxiliary's reception. Dr. Lawson from Upsala College was among the twenty-six speakers on the program. Emmy's granddaughter Emmy entertained guests with a piano recital. Presents, including a wristwatch, forty telegrams, and hundreds of birthday greetings, added to the celebration.[2] McCulloch, Emmy's longtime college friend, sent a gift. The alumni association from Rockford College mailed a congratulatory note:[3]

> No one has more beautifully carried out the hopes of the founders of this institution that its daughters who would go out into the world to make it a richer and more beautiful place in which to live. It is a source of great satisfaction to have the Emmy Evald room in the college library as a constant reminder of your loyalty and devotion to the college as well as to its ideals which you have so nobly served.[4]

The tribute suited a grand lady, who, despite her age, continued to give counsel and direction. Age did not matter much to Emmy. "I thought my mother was so old at age eighty-two, and here I am at age eighty-six, and I don't feel old, said Emmy"[5] as she recounted the story of her trip to Minnesota to receive an award. The speaker had asked who would be accepting the award on Emmy's behalf. To the crowd's amazement, she stood up quickly, chin lifted, and walked briskly toward the platform to accept her own award. Despite her dove-gray hair and rimless glasses, Emmy's tiny feet still got her where she needed to be.[6]

* * * *

The 1940s were the hardest years for the LH since its inception. Ten of its paying guests vacated in 1940—a loss of $2,700 in income. To freshen the home's appearance, half of the laundry area was converted to a kitchen, and three ranges and new fixtures were added. Double rooms were converted into singles to provide the residents with more privacy.

Blankets well-worn after ten years supplied little warmth, and bed linens were washed thin. New curtains alone required more than one thousand bolts of fabric at the cost of $300. Furthermore, the WMS had not paid for any building maintenance in nearly five years. Instead, the Emmy Evald Auxiliary picked up the tab for the remodeling.[7] Financial aid was sorely needed, but money was only one problem confronting Emmy. During World War II, the LH staff was in short supply, and there was illness among the help.

"The second cook quit, which was a hardship for such a large family," wrote Emmy. "Think of all the canning and jelly-making to be done. We have poor help. It has been impossible to get a sober man. We have hired six different men at this time."[8]

The war also reduced the number of guests at the home. "Previously we accommodated about 1,400 guests a year, last year only 573; we have had more than 15,000 visitors from thirty-one different countries, now we have none."[9]

Happy news soon boosted morale. After ten years as the resident manager of the home, Emmy was honored with a formal dinner given by the Lutheran Layman's Committee of the Lutheran Welfare Council of New York City. The occasion marked the first and only time her work was recognized by a lay organization. Dr. William Stanley, pastor of the Lutheran Church of the Good Shephard in Brooklyn, New York, introduced Emmy with the following words of praise: "Every member of the church . . . should regard it a life privilege to meet and hear this dynamic world figure who continues to guide and direct world societies of women that she has organized."[10] Emmy addressed a capacity crowd, after which refreshments were served in the church parlor. As the evening concluded, Emmy was presented with a bouquet of orchids.[11]

A testimonial gathering honored Emmy at her eighty-seventh birthday. The home's living room and adjacent halls were filled with well-wishers. She was the soul of the LH where her faithfulness and Christian spirit inspired all who lived there. But at long last, Emmy's abundant energy began to wane, and her body weakened with age and the stress of her many responsibilities. By November 1946, her health began to fail. She had lived a remarkable life through war and peace, the Great Depression, three presidential assassinations, and numerous changes from the horse and buggy to the airplane.

Knowing the end was near, Emmy's daughter Lillian flew to Reno for a quick divorce. She and Amel had been separated for more than a decade and remained cordial, but a small inheritance was at stake, and Lillian needed to secure her future.

After a month-long illness, Emmy passed away on Tuesday, December 10, 1946, leaving behind two daughters, six grandchildren, and four great-grandchildren. She was eighty-nine years old. Lillian remained at the home as the interim director until a suitable replacement could be found.

Dozens of cards and telegrams poured in from New York to California and Canada from Emmy's friends and WMS districts. A funeral was held at Gustavus Adolphus Church in New York at eight in the evening the following Thursday. Dr. J. Alfred Anderson, who worked with Emmy in New York in the search for a suitable property for the LH, provided a historical sketch. Soloist Lois Richard sang "What a Friend We Have in Jesus." Coincidentally, her father, Erland Carlsson, had helped to organize this church in 1865, completing the circle of Emmy's life.

A second funeral service happened at Immanuel Lutheran Church in Chicago the following Saturday at two thirty in the afternoon. Dr. Lawson gave the eulogy.[12] Emmy was laid to rest next to her husband, Carl, in Graceland Cemetery in Chicago.

Two memorial services honored Emmy's life. One at the Lutheran Home in New York featured a string quartet on March 2, 1947. A second service was held on June 12, 1947, at the fifty-fifth WMS annual convention in the Assembly Hall at the Municipal Auditorium in Kansas City, Missouri.

After Emmy's death, the WMS Executive Board passed a resolution, which read in part:

> Whereas it hath pleased Almighty God in his infinite wisdom to call from our midst Dr. Emmy Evald . . . a pioneer in women's work in our synod . . . who was a woman of strong conviction, [who] deeply loved the cause of missions, and by her dynamic personality inspired many to become interested in missions, and . . .
>
> Whereas many buildings on the foreign missions . . . stand today as memorials to Dr. Evald's work and leadership, . . . let it be resolved that we as a Woman's Missionary Society thank God for the great work of Dr. Emmy Evald and pray Him to bless her memory among us, and to lead us onto greater missionary endeavors.[13]

The large circle of friends who continued to remember her after so many years was a tribute to her life's work. Over the course of her lifetime, Emmy served on numerous boards and committees, and her legacy continues. A plaque in a city park in Lindsborg, Kansas, commemorates the founding of the WMS.

Emmy had lofty ambitions, and though she knew people of distinction, she remained humble. She had trials and disappointments and experienced great sorrow but faced it all with unwavering faith and courage.[14]

After her death, the WMS created the Emmy Evald memorial fund and collected $25,000, which was presented to the board of foreign missions for a home for furloughed missionaries.[15] Missionaries in China went to Hong Kong and Japan in 1949.

An Emmy Evald memorial fund of $50,000 was established in 1948 to build the Hartford Seminary Foundation in Connecticut (now Hartford Seminary), where missionaries on furlough rested and studied.[16]

In 1958, the WMS merged with the Augustana Lutheran Church Women to unify women's organizations. At that time, there were more than 1,500 missionary societies with more than 52,000 members. Approximately 120,000 children received an education through missionary schools. Financial donations reached between $8 and $9 million.[17]

Augustana Lutheran Synod merged with the Lutheran Church in America in 1962, while maintaining its emphasis on mission and social justice, and is now a part of the Evangelical Lutheran Church in America (ELCA). The *Mission Tidings* newsletter no longer exists, but multiple electronic and paper communiqués keep the ELCA women apprised of church activities and opportunities in which to serve.

The LH changed to the Inwood House, a nonprofit organization that provided housing and counseling for pregnant teens. In 2015, the building was sold to a developer for $23 million, a far cry from the $80,000 paid by the WMS in 1930.

Immanuel Lutheran Church thrives after more than 150 years. The faces of Emmy's father, Erland Carlsson, and her husband, Carl Evald, are pictured in the stained-glass windows in the sanctuary. Emmy's likeness can be found in stained glass in the narthex. She is the only woman to appear in the church windows. Today the church is culturally diverse and serves area residents in many ways, offering outreach programs such as tutoring, after-school playgroups, and neighborhood initiatives that foster better community relations.

* * * *

Some who knew Emmy's public persona thought her a mighty warrior who carried the banner for women's rights and persuaded her audiences with fiery oration.

Some knew her as a faithful and pious servant of God.

Others knew her as a loving, gentle mother to thousands of young women.

I knew her by the stories my mother told me of her amazing grandmother.

* * * *

May we all—at the end of our life journey—be safe in the arms of Jesus.

—Emmy Evald, December 1938

Author's Note

I am a half Swede whose very existence is the result of the Great Chicago Fire. Strange as that sounds, if my great-great-grandfather's church had not burnt to the ground in 1871, if the congregation had not agreed to rebuild, and if a new Swedish pastor had not been called, I would have written an entirely different book or perhaps no book at all.

My mother and her siblings were proud of their Swedish heritage and often talked of their grandmother, Emmy Evald. They told me of her trip to China, where she thwarted a robbery attempt, and of her travels to India, where she spent the day with a viper in her sleeping cot. They told of Emmy's college days with Jane Addams, her fight for women's suffrage alongside Susan B. Anthony, and of her father, Erland Carlsson.

These were grand tales indeed. But it was not until I relocated to Chicago that my interest in family history blossomed. Four generations of my family once lived in the city and are buried in Graceland Cemetery along with other notable Chicagoans, such as Louis Sullivan, Cyrus McCormick, and Marshall Field. Over time, circumstances came together in a serendipitous fashion that led me to explore my Swedish roots.

I had an opportunity to visit Emmy's home on Berwyn Avenue in Chicago while my uncle regaled me with childhood stories, and I toured the Lutheran Home in New York City. I have been to Småland, Sweden, and visited Erland Carlsson's family residence. A trip to Immanuel Lutheran Church in Chicago netted me church annuals from 1853 to 1928.

Although Emmy did not keep a diary, several relatives have shared documents, newspaper clippings, copies of her speeches, and numerous photos, some of which had been tucked away for nearly one hundred years. In addition, I spent many fruitful hours collecting data at the Lutheran (ELCA) Archives in Rosemont, Illinois (currently located in Elk Grove Village); the Chicago History Museum; and Augustana College in Rock Island, Illinois. My journey has been both interesting and rewarding.

I have found that family history becomes more important the older you are when it is frequently too late to ask questions. Time and again, those who knew the answers have either passed away or no longer remember. Emmy's work with the Woman's Missionary Society is well documented and written about in church circles, and Augustana College has produced a play about her. But her life story was not complete until I interviewed my mother, who lived with Emmy for nearly thirty years. If I had delayed in doing so, much of the information regarding Emmy's life would have been lost forever.

I would encourage you—as readers—to talk to your family and write your own memoirs for future generations. Everybody has a tale to tell. Mine is the story of Emmy Carlsson Evald.

—Sharon M. Wyman

Chronology

1851	Emmy's mother, Eva Charlotta Anderson, immigrates from Timmele, Västergötland, Sweden.
1853	Emmy's father, Rev. Erland Carlsson, immigrates from Älghult, Småland, Sweden.
	Rev. Carlsson is installed as the first preacher at Immanuel Lutheran Church at Wells and Superior in Chicago.
1855	Emmy's parents are married.
1857	Emmy Carlsson is born.
1860	Augustana College and Seminary is cofounded by Emmy's father, Rev. Erland Carlsson.
1871	Rev. Carl Evald emigrates from Örebro, Sweden.
	The new church at Sedgwick and Hobbie is destroyed in the Chicago Fire.
1875	Rev. Carl Evald is installed as the second pastor in the newly rebuilt Immanuel Lutheran Church.
1876	Rev. Evald marries Emmy's sister, Annie.
1880	Annie dies in Sweden.
1883	Emmy graduates from Rockford Seminary.
	Emmy marries Rev. Carl Evald.
1892	Emmy establishes the Woman's Missionary Society (WMS) of the Augustana Synod.
1893	The Columbian Exposition and World Congress of Religions are held in Chicago.
1895	Emmy speaks before Illinois congress in Springfield on behalf of the suffrage movement.
1898	Emmy speaks at the 30th National American Woman Suffrage Association (NAWSA) Conference in Washington, DC.

1902	Emmy speaks at the 34th NAWSA Conference and the International Woman Suffrage Conference in Washington, DC.
	Emmy speaks before the US Congress on women's suffrage.
1920	The Nineteenth Amendment is enacted, allowing women to vote.
1922	Emmy receives the Royal Vasa Medal of Honor from the King of Sweden for her mission work.
1923	Emmy's battle with Augustana College ensues.
1926	Emmy tours the WMS mission fields in China, India, and Palestine.
1935	Emmy leaves Chicago for New York City to manage the Lutheran Home for Women.
	Emmy is awarded an honorary doctorate of letters from Upsala College.
1938	Emmy's showdown with the WMS comes to a rolling boil.
1941	Rockford College dedicates an alcove in its library in honor of Emmy.
1946	Emmy dies in New York City.

Genealogy

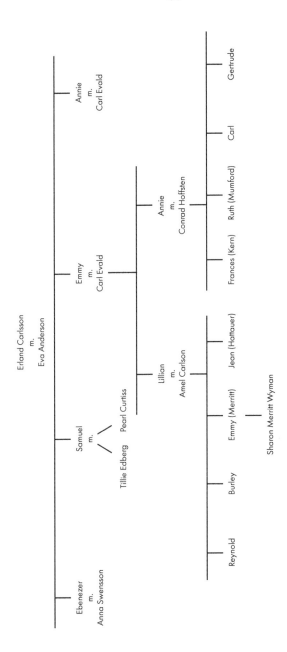

Discussion Questions

The following questions may be used with book clubs, church groups, and women's studies for further discussion and/or additional research.

Introduction: The Swedish Exodus

1. What motivated the Swedes to come to America?
2. What difficulties did they face when they arrived?
3. During the 1800s, many of the immigrants arrived from European nations. What countries do US immigrants come from today?
4. Do you know any recent immigrants? What struggles have they faced?
5. Do you have a special story about one of your ancestors who immigrated to the United States?

Chapter One: The Early Years in America (1853–1875)

1. As the daughter of a Lutheran pastor, how did Emmy's religious upbringing influence her life?
2. Was Emmy a typical preacher's kid?
3. Young Emmy earns a few pennies folding the Swedish newspaper. Do you think children should have chores? Should they earn an allowance? Should they receive guidance on how to put their money to good use?
4. How did the Chicago Fire influence the Carlsson family?
5. Emmy's parents buried more than one-half of their children. How do you think this affected their faith? Their relationship with their remaining children?

Chapter Two: Second Chances (1875–1883)

1. Emmy was a talented singer, oil painter, and teacher. How did Emmy's religion guide her to develop her talents? Does your faith or values influence your talents?

2. Emmy grew up in exciting times during the fight for women's suffrage and the Progressive movement. If she had been born in the twenty-first century, how might her life have been different?

3. Emmy was one of the first graduates from Rockford Seminary for Women. How did her college experience affect her adult years?

4. What was the traditional role for women in the nineteenth century? Do you think Emmy conformed to this role? How have the roles for women changed since Emmy's birth in 1857?

5. The Progressive movement addressed problems like worker safety, corrupt government, poverty, and sweatshops. Are today's social ills different? If so, how?

Chapter Three: The Preacher's Wife (1883–1909)

1. Temperance leader Frances Willard said that "Separated we are units of weakness, aggregated we become batteries of power." What examples of this principle do you see today?

2. Why were women of this era promoting temperance?

3. Which do you think had the greatest impact on Emmy: her faith, the era in which she lived, or her Swedish upbringing?

4. Where in Emmy's life did God play a role?

5. The women who attended the World Congress of Religions, specifically the Lutheran women's gathering, spoke about women's roles in the church. What roles do women assume in churches today? What obstacles do they face?

Chapter Four: Getting the Vote (1895–1920)

1. How do you think the Civil War and World War I influenced the attitudes toward suffrage?

2. Do you think the WMS slogan, "Christian patriotism keeps the glow in Old Glory," would be acceptable today?

3. In what ways did Emmy's leadership skills promote women's equality?

4. Can you think of a twenty-first-century woman who exemplifies Emmy's spirit?

5. What were the arguments against women's suffrage?

6. What characteristics did Susan B. Anthony and other suffragists have in common?

Chapter Five: The Woman's Missionary Society (1892–1935)

1. Discuss the following slogans from the WMS newsletter: "The thermometer of a man's character is his attitude toward women," and "Woman's status determines to a very large extent the character of her nation."
2. What kinds of missionary work happens in society today?
3. Can you imagine sponsoring fifty orphans in France? How did Emmy amass the funds?
4. What problems did the missionaries encounter in China and India?
5. Investigate women's rights in China and India today.

Chapter Six: Triumphs and Turbulence (1920–1930)

1. Emmy becomes embroiled in a fight with Augustana College over the location of the women's dorm. What does this say about her? Does it take a strong personality to be a "mover and a shaker"?
2. Emmy loses her fight with Augustana. Do you think her decisions were the right ones? What helps you make important decisions?
3. Why do you think Emmy decided to travel to China, India, and the Holy Land despite the dangers?
4. How does history repeat itself in these countries? What are the difficulties that young women in these regions face today?
5. What did Emmy mean when she said, "The opposition is to Christianity not to Christ. The church is a foreign institution. We must let them know that they can accept Christ and reject Western civilization"?

Chapter Seven: Life at Berwyn Avenue (1930–1940)

1. Emmy entertains her grandchildren by taking them on several outings to the zoo and other places. What special times do you enjoy with your grandchildren or did you enjoy with your grandparents? How can grandparents strengthen the bond with their grandchildren when they do not live nearby?

2. Emmy's Christmas dinner includes many Swedish foods. What traditional or special foods can be found on your holiday table?
3. Several church members at Immanuel committed suicide after the stock market crash of 1929. Does a strong faith help overcome external problems? What assistance can be found within your community to aid those in need?
4. Economic issues contributed to the failed marriage of Emmy's daughter. What issues contribute to today's divorce rate?
5. Emmy receives many honors and still describes herself as "a little tool in my Master's hand." Do you think it is easy to remain humble when you have achieved such importance? Why or why not?

Chapter Eight: The Lutheran Home for Women (1930–1935)

1. What obstacles did Emmy overcome in finding a suitable building for the Lutheran Home?
2. How would you feel after spending the WMS money if you could not renovate the property?
3. Did Emmy's hands-on approach to the remodeling of the building illustrate good management?
4. What was your reaction to Emmy's granddaughter's essay regarding the Lutheran Home?
5. What problems do young women today face when moving out on their own for the first time?

Chapter Nine: The Showdown (1935–1938)

1. What was the root cause of Emmy's conflict with the WMS Executive Board? Can you see both points of view?
2. Was Emmy too old to be managing the Lutheran Home?
3. Many people came to Emmy's defense. What does this say about her abilities to direct?
4. When the WMS Executive Board backed down, were you surprised? Why do you think they changed their minds and returned home?
5. Why do you think Emmy was so energetic up until her late eighties? Do you think she ignored the normal aches and pains of an aging body?

Epilogue

1. What did you think of the author's description of her great-grandmother?
2. How would you describe the women in your family?
3. How much do you know about your ancestors? Who could you ask to find out more?
4. We inherit physical characteristics from family members. What personality traits or talents have you also inherited?
5. What will you pass on to your children?

For Further Reading

Following is a list of resources for readers seeking additional information on Emmy Evald and the times in which she lived.

Books

Anderson, Philip J. and Dag Blanck, eds. *Swedish-American Life in Chicago.* Urbana: University of Illinois Press, 1992.

Arden, G. Everett. *Augustana Heritage: A History of the Augustana Lutheran Church.* Rock Island, IL: Augustana Press, 1963.

Badger, R. Reid. *The Great American Fair: The World's Columbian Exposition and American Culture.* Chicago: Nelson-Hall, 1979.

Beijbom, Ulf. *Swedes in Chicago: A Demographic and Social Study of the 1846–1880 Immigration.* Translated by Donald Brown. Vaxjo, Sweden: Davidsons Boktryckeri AB, 1971.

Bergendoff, Conrad. *Augustana . . . A Profession of Faith: A History of Augustana College, 1860–1935.* Rock Island, IL: Augustana College Library, 1969.

Buechler, Steven M. *The Transformation of the Woman Suffrage Movement: The Case of Illinois, 1850–1920.* New Brunswick, NJ: Rutgers University Press, 1986.

Carlberg, Gustav, ed. *Thirty Years in China—1905–1935: The Story of the Augustana Synod Mission in the Province of Honan as Told by Missionaries.* Board of Foreign Missions of Augustana Synod, 1937.

Coble, Alana Erickson. *Cleaning Up: The Transformation of Domestic Service in Twentieth Century New York City.* New York: Routledge/Taylor and Francis Group, 2006.

Diliberto, Gioia. *A Useful Woman: The Early Life of Jane Addams*. New York: Lisa Drew Book/Scribner, 1999.

Flanagan, Maureen A. *Seeing with Their Hearts: Chicago Women and the Vision of the Good City, 1871–1933*. Princeton, NJ: Princeton University Press, 2002.

Gifford, Hartland H. and Arland J. Hultgren, eds. *The Heritage of Augustana: Essays on the Life and Legacy of the Augustana Lutheran Church*. Minneapolis: Kirk House Publishers, 2004.

Grossman, James R., Ann Durkin Keating, and Janice L. Reiff, eds. *The Encyclopedia of Chicago*. Chicago: University of Chicago Press, 2004.

Gustafson, Anita Olson. *Swedish Chicago: The Shaping of an Immigrant Community, 1880-1920*. DeKalb, IL: NIU Press, 2018.

Hall, George F. *The Missionary Spirit in the Augustana Church*. Davenport, IA: Wagners Printers, 1984.

Heise, Kenan. *The Chicagoization of America: 1893–1917*. Evanston, IL: Chicago Historical Bookworks, 1990.

Holcombe, Arthur N. *The Spirit of the Chinese Revolution*. New York: Knopf, 1930.

Holli, Melvin G., and Peter d'A. Jones, eds. *Ethnic Chicago: A Multicultural Portrait*. Grand Rapids, MI: Eerdmans, 1995.

Holmquist, Thomas N. *Pioneer Cross: Swedish Settlements Along the Smoky Hill Bluffs*. Hillsboro, KS: Hearth Publishing, 1994.

Jensson, J. C. *American Lutheran Biographies*. Milwaukee: Houtkamp and Sons, 1880.

Johnson, Lani L. *Led by the Spirit: A History of Lutheran Church Women*. Philadelphia: Lutheran Church Women, 1980.

Keating, Ann Durkin. *Building Chicago: Suburban Developers & the Creation of a Divided Metropolis*. Columbus: Ohio State University Press, 1988.

Keiser, John H. *Building for the Centuries: Illinois 1865–1898*. Urbana: University of Illinois Press, 1977.

Kent, Eliza F. *Converting Women: Gender and Protestant Christianity in Colonial South India*. New York: Oxford University Press, 2004.

Kraditor, Aileen S. *Up from the Pedestal*. Chicago: Quadrangle Books, 1968.

Kublin, Hyman. *China*. Boston: Houghton Mifflin, 1972.

Latourette, Kenneth Scott. *A History of Christian Missions in China*. New York: Russell and Russell, 1967.

Lemons, J. Stanley. *The Woman Citizen: Social Feminism in the 1920s*. Chicago: University of Illinois Press, 1973.

Lindquist, Emory. *Shepherd of an Immigrant People: The Story of Erland Carlsson*. Rock Island, IL: Augustana Historical Society, 1978.

Ljungmark, Lars. *Swedish Exodus*. Translated by Kermit B. Westerberg. Carbondale: Southern Illinois Press, 1979.

Mayer, Harold M., and Richard C. Wade. *Chicago: Growth of a Metropolis*. Chicago: University of Chicago Press, 1969.

Miller, Donald L. *City of the Century: The Epic of Chicago and the Making of America*. New York: Simon and Schuster, 1996.

Muccigrosso, Robert. *Celebrating the New World: Chicago's Columbian Exposition of 1893*. Chicago: American Ways Series, 1993.

Olsen, Ernst W., ed. *History of the Swedes in Illinois*. Chicago: Engberg-Holmberg Publishing, 1908.

Reitano, Joanne. *The Restless City: A Short History of New York from Colonial Times to the Present*. New York: Routledge/Taylor and Francis Group, 2006.

Ronnegard, Sam. *Prairie Shepherd: Lars Paul Esbjörn and the Beginnings of the Augustana Lutheran Church*. Rock Island, IL: Augustana Book Concern, 1952.

Ruth, Janice E., and Evelyn Sinclair. *Women of the Suffrage Movement*. Women Who Dare. San Francisco: Pomegranate Communications, 2006.

Schultz, Rima Lunin and Adele Hast, eds. *Women Building Chicago 1790–1990: A Biographical Dictionary*. Bloomington: Indiana University Press, 2001.

Sizer, Nancy Faust, and Rebecca S. Rudd. *China: A Brief History*. Wellesley Hills, MA: Independent School Press, 1981.

Smith, Page. *Daughters of the Promised Land: Women in American History*. Boston: Little, Brown and Company, 1970.

Spinney, Robert G. *City of Big Shoulders: A History of Chicago.* Dekalb: Northern Illinois University Press, 2000.

Wheeler, Adade Mitchell. *The Roads They Made: Women in Illinois History.* Chicago: Charles Kerr Publishing, 1977.

Websites

Harper, Ida Husted, ed. *The History of Woman Suffrage, vol. 5: 1900–1920.* New York: National American Woman Suffrage Association, 1922. Accessed March 20, 2017. http://archive.org/details/historyofwomansu05stanuoft.

Sorensen, Mark W. "Ahead of Their Time: A Brief History of Woman Suffrage in Illinois." *Illinois Periodicals Online.* Accessed March 20, 2017. http://www .lib.niu.edu/2004/ih110604half.html.

US House Committee on the Judiciary. *Woman Suffrage: Hearing before the Committee*, 57th Cong., 1st sess., February 18, 1902. Accessed March 20, 2017. https://www.loc.gov/resource/rbnawsa.n4776/.

US Senate Select Committee on Woman Suffrage. W*oman Suffrage: Hearing . . . on the joint resolution (S.R. 53) proposing an amendment to the Constitution of the United States, extending the right of suffrage to women*, 57th Cong., 1st sess., February 18, 1902. Accessed March 20, 2017. https:// www.loc.gov/resource/rbnawsa.n4783/.

Notes

Introduction: The Swedish Exodus

1. Anita Olson Gustafson, "Swedes," in *The Encyclopedia of Chicago*, eds. James R. Grossman, Ann Durkin Keating, and Janice L. Reiff (Chicago: University of Chicago Press, 2004), 805.
2. Ernst W. Olsen, ed., *History of the Swedes in Illinois* (Chicago: Engberg-Holmberg Publishing, 1908), 13.
3. Ulf Beijbom, *Swedes in Chicago: A Demographic and Social Study of the 1846–1880 Immigration*, trans. Donald Brown (Vaxjo, Sweden: Davidsons Boktryckeri AB, 1971), 29.
4. Thomas N. Holmquist, *Pioneer Cross: Swedish Settlements Along the Smoky Hill Bluffs* (Hillsboro, KS: Hearth Publishing, 1994), 6–8.
5. Olsen, *History of the Swedes*, 4–5.
6. Olsen, 5.
7. Beijbom, *Swedes in Chicago*, 148.
8. Holmquist, *Pioneer Cross*, 20.
9. Holmquist, 22.
10. Holmquist, 25.
11. Beijbom, *Swedes in Chicago*, 313.
12. Lars Ljungmark, *Swedish Exodus*, trans. Kermit B. Westerberg (Carbondale: Southern Illinois Press, 1979), 76.
13. Beijbom, *Swedes in Chicago*, 76–77.
14. Emory Lindquist, *Shepherd of an Immigrant People: The Story of Erland Carlsson* (Rock Island, IL: Augustana Historical Society, 1978), 213.
15. Ljungmark, *Swedish Exodus*, 82.
16. Olsen, *History of the Swedes*, 466.
17. Harold M. Mayer and Richard C. Wade, *Chicago: Growth of a Metropolis* (Chicago: University of Chicago Press, 1969), 32.
18. Philip J. Anderson and Dag Blanck, eds., *Swedish-American Life in Chicago* (Urbana: University of Illinois Press, 1992), 104.
19. Anderson and Blanck, 104.
20. Ann Durkin Keating, *Building Chicago: Suburban Developers & the Creation of a Divided Metropolis* (Columbus: Ohio State University Press, 1988), 34.
21. Beijbom, *Swedes in Chicago*, 101–102.
22. Mayer and Wade, *Chicago: Growth of a Metropolis*, 81.
23. Mayer and Wade, 26.
24. Beijbom, *Swedes in Chicago*, 145.

25. Robert G. Spinney, *City of Big Shoulders: A History of Chicago* (Dekalb: Northern Illinois University Press, 2000), 140.
26. Beijbom, *Swedes in Chicago*, 64.
27. Beijbom, 100.

Chapter One: The Early Years in America (1853–1875)

1. Beijbom, *Swedes in Chicago*, 237.
2. Sam Ronnegard, *Prairie Shepherd: Lars Paul Esbjörn and the Beginnings of the Augustana Lutheran Church* (Rock Island, IL: Augustana Book Concern, 1952), 100, 113.
3. Lindquist, *Immigrant People*, 24.
4. Emmy Evald, "Early Days of the Augustana Synod in Chicago" (speech to the Pastor's Association, June 6, 1932).
5. Lindquist, *Immigrant People*, 61.
6. Beijbom, *Swedes in Chicago*, 355.
7. Anderson and Blanck, *Swedish-American Life*, 6.
8. John H. Keiser, *Building for the Centuries: Illinois 1865–1898* (Urbana: University of Illinois Press, 1977), 304.
9. Olsen, *History of the Swedes*, 469.
10. Lindquist, *Immigrant People*, 41, 47.
11. *The Story of Immanuel Lutheran Church 1853–1928* (Chicago: Evangelical Lutheran Immanuel Church, 1928), 12.
12. *Story of Immanuel Lutheran*, 15.
13. Evald, "Early Days" (speech).
14. Lindquist, *Immigrant People*, 82.
15. Evald, "Early Days" (speech).
16. Lindquist, *Immigrant People*, 82, 84.
17. Evald, "Early Days" (speech).
18. Keiser, *Building for the Centuries*, 310.
19. "The Story of Augustana College and Theological Seminary," in *After Seventy-Five Years 1860–1935* (Rock Island, IL: Augustana Book Concern, 1935), 31.
20. Emmy Evald, "A Child's Recollection of the Pioneer Days of 1860 and 1864" (speech, n.d.).
21. Evald, speech.
22. Gustafson, "Swedes," 805.
23. *Story of Immanuel Lutheran*, 16.
24. *Story of Immanuel Lutheran*, 18.
25. *Story of Immanuel Lutheran*, 17.
26. Beijbom, *Swedes in Chicago*, 68.
27. *Story of Immanuel Lutheran*, 18.
28. Lindquist, *Immigrant People*, 64.
29. Lindquist, 65.
30. *Story of Immanuel Lutheran*, 18.
31. *Story of Immanuel Lutheran*, 18.
32. *Story of Immanuel Lutheran*, 18.
33. *Story of Immanuel Lutheran*, 20.
34. *Story of Immanuel Lutheran*, 69.
35. *Story of Immanuel Lutheran*, 124.
36. Evald, "Early Days" (speech).

Chapter Two: Second Chances (1875–1883)

1. Lindquist, *Immigrant People*, 181.
2. Lindquist, 183.
3. *The Lutheran Companion* 51 (February 17, 1943).
4. Olsen, *History of the Swedes*, 157–158.
5. Lindquist, *Immigrant People*, 184.
6. Emmy Evald, "Memories of Andover" (speech, Jenny Lind Chapel Founders' Day Celebration, Andover, IL, April 24, 1938).
7. *The Lutheran Companion* 51 (February 17, 1943).
8. G. Everett Arden, *Augustana Heritage: A History of the Augustana Lutheran Church* (Rock Island, IL: Augustana Press, 1963), 207–208.
9. Olsen, *History of the Swedes*, 208.
10. Peter Peterson, "Mrs. Evald's Church Activities" (speech, Chicago, January 10, 1922).
11. *Daily Gazette*, Rock Island, IL, May 17, 1879.
12. Lindquist, *Immigrant People*, 172.
13. Lindquist, 188–190.
14. Lindquist, 187.
15. The *Lutheran Companion* (November 25, 1937).
16. Lindquist, *Immigrant People*, 188.
17. Maureen A. Flanagan, *Seeing with Their Hearts: Chicago Women and the Vision of the Good City, 1871–1933* (Princeton, NJ: Princeton University Press, 2002), 35.
18. *Catalogue, Rockford Seminary, 1882–1883* (Rockford, IL: Rockford Seminary, 1883).
19. Gioia Diliberto, *A Useful Woman: The Early Life of Jane Addams* (New York: Lisa Drew Book/Scribner, 1999), 61–65.
20. Diliberto, 63–64.
21. Diliberto, 61–65.
22. Aileen S. Kraditor, *Up from the Pedestal* (Chicago: Quadrangle Books, 1968), 10.
23. Diliberto, *A Useful Woman*, 60.
24. Anderson and Blanck, *Swedish-American Life*, 89.
25. Keiser, *Building for the Centuries*, 8.

Chapter Three: The Preacher's Wife (1883–1909)

1. Beijbom, *Swedes in Chicago*, 9.
2. Melvin G. Holli and Peter d'A. Jones, eds., *Ethnic Chicago: A Multicultural Portrait* (Grand Rapids, MI: Eerdmans, 1995), 111.
3. Spinney, *City of Big Shoulders*, 66.
4. Anderson and Blanck, *Swedish-American Life*, 50–51.
5. J. C. Jensson, *American Lutheran Biographies* (Milwaukee: Houtkamp and Sons, 1880), 207.
6. *Seventy-Five Years of Christian Service in Minneapolis* (Minneapolis: Augustana Evangelical Lutheran Church, n.d.), 10–11.
7. *The Lutheran Journal*, April 8, 1909, 112.
8. John Telleen, "Sermon delivered to the Immanuel Lutheran Church Sunday School at the Memorial Service (March 19, 1909)," in *Teol. Doktor Carl A. Evald*, comp. Emmy Evald (Chicago: 1910), 92.
9. R. F. Weidner, "Dr. Evald and Chicago Lutheran Theological Seminary," in *Teol. Doktor Carl A. Evald*, comp. Emmy Evald (Chicago: 1910), 77–78.
10. Lindquist, *Immigrant People*, 184.
11. *Story of Immanuel Lutheran*, 31.
12. Olsen, *History of the Swedes*, 471.

13. Annie Hoffsten, (essay, n.d.), 1.
14. Conrad O. Bengtson, "Doctor Emmy Evald" (speech, n.d.), 5.
15. *Story of Immanuel Lutheran*, 24.
16. *Story of Immanuel Lutheran*, 26.
17. *Story of Immanuel Lutheran*, 31.
18. *Story of Immanuel Lutheran*, 31.
19. Olsen, *History of the Swedes*, 539.
20. Lennart Johnsson, "The Global Impact of Emmy Evald and the Women's Missionary Society," *Augustana Heritage Association* (2006): 10, accessed November 3, 2016, http://augustanaheritage.org/Johnsson%20on%20%20Emmy%20Evald.pdf.
21. George F. Hall, "Augustana's Evald: Missions Energy," *The Lutheran*, April 1, 1987, 9.
22. Doris Hedeen Spong, "Led by the Spirit," *Augustana Heritage Newsletter* 3, no. 3 (March 1998): 2.
23. Kathleen S. Hurty, "Emmy Carlsson Evald: Passion, Power, and Persistence," in *The Heritage of Augustana: Essays on the Life and Legacy of the Augustana Lutheran Church*, eds. Hartland H. Gifford and Arland J. Hultgren (Minneapolis: Kirk House Publishers, 2004), 256.
24. Emmy Evald, personal papers.
25. Hurty, 252.
26. Evald, personal papers.
27. G. A. Barndelle, "The Woman's Missionary Society, All Hail!" *The Lutheran Companion* (May 28, 1932).
28. Hurty, 256.
29. *Mission Tidings* 13, no. 2 (July 1919): 19.
30. Emmy Evald, "Why a Woman's Missionary Society," *The Lutheran Companion* (May 28, 1932): 683.
31. Arden, *Augustana Heritage*, 211–213.
32. *Mission Tidings* 13, 19.
33. "Our Day of Triumph," *The Daily Inter Ocean*, vol. 22, no. 39, May 2, 1893.
34. "The Best Exhibit of Hall," *The Daily Inter Ocean*, May 20, 1893.
35. Olsen, 161.
36. R. Reid Badger, *The Great American Fair: The World's Columbian Exposition and American Culture* (Chicago: Nelson-Hall, 1979), 79.
37. Isabelle Laning Cander, "Illinois Women's Clubs," *The Woman's Journal (Boston)*, April 20, 1895.
38. *The Sunday Inter Ocean*, vol. 23, no. 9, April 2, 1893.
39. Frank Tennyson Neely, *Neely's History of the Parliament of Religions and Religious Congresses at the World's Columbian Exposition* (n.p., 1893), 25.
40. Neely, 35.
41. Badger, *Great American Fair*, 98.
42. Badger, 101.
43. Badger, 101–102.
44. Neely, *Parliament of Religions*, 201.
45. Badger, *Great American Fair*, 102.
46. Evald, personal papers.
47. Bengtson, "Doctor Emmy Evald" (speech).
48. J. W. Hanson, ed., *The World's Congress of Religions: The addresses and papers delivered before the parliament and an abstract of the congresses . . . at the World's Columbian Exposition* (Chicago: W. B. Conkey, 1894), 1032–1034.
49. "Their Last Sessions, *The Daily Inter Ocean*, n.d.

50. Donald L. Miller, *City of the Century: The Epic of Chicago and the Making of America* (New York: Simon and Schuster, 1996), 550.
51. *Chicago Daily Tribune*, October 26, 1893.
52. Evald, personal papers.
53. Alvina Marie Sandholm, "A Study of the Children's Receiving Home, Maywood, Illinois; An Institution for the Care of Dependent Children" (master's thesis, Loyola University Chicago, 1952), accessed March 13, 2017, http://ecommons.luc.edu /luc_theses/1251.
54. *Story of Immanuel Lutheran*, 32.
55. "Swedish Lutheran Church Holds a Golden Jubilee," *Chicago Daily Tribune*, January 16, 1903.
56. Olsen, *History of the Swedes*, 473.
57. *The Immanuel Woman's Home 1907–1933* (Chicago: Windahl Print, n.d.), 12.
58. *Immanuel Woman's Home 1907–1933*, 9.
59. *Immanuel Woman's Home 1907–1933*, 24.
60. *The Immanuel Woman's Home: 50 Years of Service Anniversary* (Chicago: 1957), 1–2.
61. *The Immanuel Woman's Home: 50 Years of Service Anniversary*, 2.
62. *The Immanuel Woman's Home, Thirty Years of Service* (Chicago: 1907–1937), 17.
63. *Immanuel Woman's Home 1907–1933*, 2, 11, 22–29.
64. *Chicago Daily Tribune*, May 24, 1908.
65. John Telleen, "Memorial Service," 91.
66. G. H. Gerberding, "Reflections of the Death and Burial of a Minister," *The Lutheran Journal*, April 8, 1909, 109–111.
67. Bengtson, "Doctor Emmy Evald" (speech).
68. *Chicago Daily Tribune*, May 26, 1909.
69. Ruth Hoffsten Mumford, "Remembrances of Emmy Evald" (essay, n.p., n.d.).

Chapter Four: Getting the Vote (1895–1920)

1. *The Daily Inter Ocean*, (n.d.)
2. *The Housekeeper*, November 15, 1895.
3. Mark W. Sorensen, "Ahead of Their Time: A Brief History of Woman Suffrage in Illinois," *Illinois Periodicals Online*, accessed March 20, 2017, http://www.lib.niu.edu /2004/ih110604half.html.
4. Jeanne Carpenter, "Sixty Years of Service," The Woman Republican (n.p. n.d.) 6.
5. Catherine Waugh McCulloch, letter to Mrs. Rutledge, March 4, 1939.
6. "Swedish-American Women's League," *Chicago Times Herald*, October 15, 1896.
7. *Chicago Daily Tribune*, February 13, 1898.
8. *Chicago Daily Tribune*, October 18, 1896.
9. *Chicago Daily Tribune*, 1896.
10. *Chicago Daily Tribune*, 1896
11. *Chicago Daily Tribune*, 1896
12. "Clubs Open New Season," *Chicago Daily Tribune*, October 7, 1900.
13. George F. Hall, *The Missionary Spirit in the Augustana Church* (Davenport, IA: Wagners Printers, 1984), 18.
14. Carpenter, "Sixty Years of Service," 6.
15. *Proceedings of the Thirtieth Annual Convention of the National American Woman Suffrage Association and the Celebrations of the Fiftieth Anniversary of the First Woman's Rights Convention* (Washington, DC, February 13–19, 1898), 7, 59, 64.

16. Ida Husted Harper, ed., *The History of Woman Suffrage, vol. 5: 1900–1920* (New York: National American Woman Suffrage Association, 1922), accessed March 20, 2017, http://archive.org/details/historyofwomansu05stanuoft, 23.
17. Harper, 24.
18. Harper, 51.
19. Harper, 52.
20. *Report, First International Woman Suffrage Conference* (Washington, DC, February 1902), 113–116.
21. *Report,* 4.
22. House Committee on the Judiciary, *Woman Suffrage: Hearing before the Committee,* 57th Cong., 1st sess., February 18, 1902, accessed March 20, 2017, https://www.loc.gov/resource/rbnawsa.n4776/, 6.
23. House Committee, *Woman Suffrage,* 6–7.
24. House Committee, 8–9.
25. House Committee, 23.
26. Senate Select Committee on Woman Suffrage, *Woman Suffrage: Hearing . . . on the joint resolution (S.R. 53) proposing an amendment to the Constitution of the United States, extending the right of suffrage to women,* 57th Cong., 1st sess., February 18, 1902, accessed March 20, 2017, https://www.loc.gov/resource/rbnawsa.n4783/, 26.
27. Senate Select Committee, *Woman Suffrage,* 34–35.
28. Senate Select Committee, 39.
29. Harper, *History of Woman Suffrage,* 11.
30. Harper, 46.
31. "Equal Suffrage Convention," *Chicago Daily,* October 7, 1900.
32. "Women Meet at Joliet," *Chicago Daily,* October 7, 1903.
33. *Chicago Sunday Times Herald,* October 6, 1895.
34. Kraditor, *Up from the Pedestal,* 120.
35. Adade Mitchell Wheeler, "Conflict in Illinois: Woman Suffrage Movement of 1913," *Journal of the Illinois State Historical Society* 76 (summer 1983): 95–114.
36. Kraditor, *Up from the Pedestal,* 121.
37. "Here Come the Motoring Militant Suffragettes," *Chicago Daily Tribune,* July 10, 1910.
38. Wheeler, "Conflict in Illinois," 95.
39. "Mrs. Catt Puts Suffrage Foes in Three Classes," *Chicago Daily Tribune,* May 8, 1916.
40. Carpenter, "Sixty Years of Service," 7–8.
41. Catherine Waugh McCulloch, letter to Emmy Evald, September 6, 1937.

Chapter Five: The Woman's Missionary Society (1892–1935)

1. *Mission Tidings* 8, no. 1 (June–July 1913): 1, 2, 23.
2. S. G. Hagglund, "The Woman's Missionary Society," in *After Seventy-Five Years 1860–1935* (Rock Island, IL: Augustana Book Concern, 1935), 226.
3. Anabel Parker McCann, *New York Sun,* March 2, 1932.
4. Jane Telleen, "The Women's Missionary Society," in *The Heritage of Augustana: Essays on the Life and Legacy of the Augustana Lutheran Church,* eds. Hartland H. Gifford and Arland J. Hultgren (Minneapolis: Kirk House Publishers, 2004), 242.
5. Johnsson, "Women's Missionary Society," 8.
6. *Mission Tidings* 6, no. 5 (October 1911): 12.
7. Evald, "Why a Woman's Missionary Society."
8. Arden, *Augustana Heritage,* 213.

9. Alma Swensson, "Greetings from Mission Tidings," *The Lutheran Companion* (May 28, 1932): 684.
10. *Mission Tidings* 13, no. 2 (July 1918): 14.
11. Minutes of the WMS Executive Committee, Immanuel Lutheran Church, Chicago, September 7, 1907.
12. Marie Telleen, "Woman's Work in Persia," *Mission Tidings* 14, no. 5 (October 1919): 11.
13. Spong, "Led by the Spirit," 3.
14. Spong, 1–3.
15. *Mission Tidings* 8, no. 6 (November 1913): 10.
16. *Mission Tidings* 13, no. 1 (June 1918): 3.
17. Arthur Johnson, "National and International Relationships of the Augustana Synod," in *After Seventy-Five Years 1860–1935* (Rock Island, IL: Augustana Book Concern, 1935), 84.
18. Johnson, 1, 8.
19. *Mission Tidings* 13, nos. 3–4 (August–September 1918): 13.
20. *Mission Tidings* 13, nos. 3–4, 13.
21. Ruth Benson, *From Acorns Small* (Chicago: Augustana Lutheran Church Women, n.d.), 12.
22. *Mission Tidings* 13, no. 2 (July 1918): 15.
23. *Mission Tidings* 13, no. 12 (May 1919): 13.
24. Spong, "Led by the Spirit," 1–3.
25. *Mission Tidings* 7, no. 1 (June 1912): 4.
26. *Mission Tidings* 7, no. 2 (July 1912): 7.
27. *Mission Tidings* 7, no. 2, 7.
28. Minutes of the WMS Executive Committee, Immanuel Lutheran Church, Chicago, July 28, 1908.
29. "Synod Women Plan Nilsson Memorial Here," *The Rockford Register-Gazette*, June 8, 1929.
30. Evald, personal papers.
31. *Mission Tidings* 12, no. 3 (August 1917): 16.
32. Irving Park Lutheran Church bulletin (January 31, 1926).
33. *Mission Tidings* 6 (July 1911): 25.
34. O. J. Johnson, "Our Missions Abroad," in *After Seventy-Five Years 1860–1935* (Rock Island, IL: Augustana Book Concern, 1935), 200.
35. *Mission Tidings* 5, no. 10 (March 1911): 13.
36. *Mission Tidings* 7, no. 3 (August 1912): 14.
37. *Mission Tidings* 7, no. 3, 14.
38. *Mission Tidings* 8, no. 7 (December 1913): 3.
39. *Mission Tidings* 7, no. 12 (March 1913): 3.
40. *Mission Tidings* 18, no. 12 (May 1919): 4.
41. *Mission Tidings* 8, no. 12 (May 1914): 6.
42. *Mission Tidings* 7, no. 2 (July 1912): 7.
43. *Mission Tidings* 12, no. 3 (August 1917): 16.
44. Among Ourselves, *Mission Tidings* (n.d.).
45. Evald, personal papers.
46. *Mission Tidings* 9, no. 10 (March 1915): 3.
47. May C. Mellander, "Our Mission in China," *Mission Tidings* 14, nos. 3–4 (August–September 1919): 1–2.
48. Lillie Starbranch Benson, *Fran Kina* [From China], *Mission Tidings* 9, no. 10 (March 1915): 2.

49. David C. Edwins, "Come With Me: The Augustana Mission in Honan Province, China," *Augustana Heritage Association* (2006): 2–3, accessed December 30, 2016, http://augustanaheritage.org/Edwins%20on%20China.pdf.
50. Lillie Benson, *Fran Kina*, 2.
51. Ruth Vikner Gamelin, "Our China Mission: A Child's Experiences," *Augustana Heritage Association*, adapted from her memoir, *Growing Up in China* (2006): 2, accessed December 30, 2016, http://augustanaheritage.augustana.edu/R%20 Gamelin%20Paper%20Rev.pdf.
52. Gamelin, 2.
53. *Our Second Decade in China 1915 to 1925: Sketches and Reminiscences, as told by the Missionaries of the Augustana Synod Mission in the Province of Honan* (The Board of Foreign Missions of the Augustan Synod, n.d.), 155.
54. *Mission Tidings* 14, nos. 3–4 (August–September 1919): 1.
55. Evald, personal papers.
56. *Mission Tidings* 7, no. 4 (September 12, 1912): 5.
57. *Mission Tidings* 8, no. 8 (January 1914): 2.
58. *Mission Tidings* 9, no. 10 (March 1915): 1.
59. Gamelin, "Our China Mission," 1.
60. *Mission Tidings* 7, no. 11 (April 1913): 20.
61. *Mission Tidings* 7, no. 12 (March 1913): 9.
62. "Woman's Missionary Society, Evangelical Lutheran Augustana Synod" (speech, n.p., n.d.).
63. *Mission Tidings* 7, no. 12 (March 1913): 10.
64. *Mission Tidings* 14, nos. 3–4 (August–September 1919): 3.
65. *Chicago American,* June 15, 1933.
66. Marie Telleen, "Woman's Work in Persia," *Mission Tidings* 6, no. 5 (October 1911): 12–13.
67. Telleen, 12–13.
68. Evald, personal papers.
69. Emma R. Schmid, "What is Our Lutheran Church doing for Porto Rico," *Mission Tidings* 9, no. 6 (November 1914): 2.
70. *Mission Tidings* 30, no. 10 (April 1936): 229.
71. "Go Tell" (n.p., n.d.), 9.
72. "Mrs. Emmy Evald, 77, Seeks New Work in Mission Field," *The Minneapolis Journal,* June 9, 1934.
73. *Proceedings of the Annual WMS Conference* (1924), 261.
74. Mrs. P. Peterson, *Mission Tidings* 12, no. 9 (February 1918): 4.
75. Evald, personal papers.
76. *Tenth Anniversary: Augustana Lutheran Mission Home: 1924–1934* (Evangelical Lutheran Augustana Synod, n.d.), 1–2.
77. *Tenth Anniversary*, 6–8.
78. Benson, *Acorns Small*, 7.
79. Mrs. Charles L. Fay, "The Benefit of a Woman's Missionary Federation of the General Council," *Mission Tidings* 5, no. 8 (January 15, 1910).

Chapter Six: Triumph and Turbulence (1920–1930)

1. Bengtson, "Doctor Emmy Evald" (speech).
2. "Lutheran Women's Activities," *The Lutheran* (February 9, 1922): 12.
3. "Fortieth Anniversary Jubilee," *The Lutheran Companion* (May 28, 1932): 682.
4. "Fortieth Anniversary Jubilee," 683.

5. Emmy Evald, Among Ourselves, *Mission Tidings*, no. 7 (December 1925): 9.
6. *Our Second Decade in China*, 199.
7. Evald, personal papers.
8. Gustav Carlberg, ed., *Thirty Years in China—1905–1935: The Story of the Augustana Synod Mission in the Province of Honan as Told by Missionaries* (Board of Foreign Missions of Augustana Synod, 1937), 22.
9. Carlberg, 23.
10. Women's Mission Society Survey of 35 Years, Calendar #9.
11. *Chicago Daily Tribune*, January 1, 1924.
12. *Our Second Decade in China*, 74.
13. Evald, personal papers.
14. Minutes of the WMS Executive Board, Chicago, August 27, 1926.
15. *Proceedings of the WMS 42nd Annual Conference* (June 14–17, 1933), 273–274.
16. *New York Sun*, April 24, 1936.
17. McCann, *New York Sun*, March 2, 1932.
18. *Portland (Maine) Press Herald*, October 19, 1928.
19. *New York Sun*, April 24, 1937.
20. McCann, *New York Sun*, March 2, 1932.
21. *Our Second Decade in China*, 85–89.
22. *Tenth Anniversary*, 9.
23. Rev. John L. Benson, letter to the Woman's Missionary Society, Hsuchow, Honan, China, January 5, 1927.
24. *Portland (Maine) Press Herald*, October 19, 1928.
25. Minutes of the WMS Executive Board, Chicago, August 27, 1926.
26. Carlberg, *Thirty Years in China*, 26.
27. Minutes of the WMS Executive Board, Chicago, February 27, 1928.
28. Evald, "Early Days" (speech).
29. Conrad Bergendoff, *Augustana . . . A Profession of Faith: A History of Augustana College, 1860–1935* (Rock Island, IL: Augustana College Library, 1969), 153–156.
30. "Plea for Our Daughters," Woman's Building Campaign at Augustana (n.p., n.d.).
31. Emmy Evald, Among Ourselves, *Mission Tidings* 16, no. 2–3 (July–August 1921): 31.
32. "Plea for Our Daughters."
33. "Big Drive Launched for Ladies' Hall," *The Augustana Observer*, September 23, 1921.
34. "Plea for Our Daughters."
35. *Mission Tidings* (1922): 233.
36. Woman's Mission Board Chairman, letter to Joseph Anderson, March 30, 1922.
37. *Mission Tidings* (1922): 235.
38. *Mission Tidings* (1922): 233.
39. Jane Telleen, "Women's Missionary Society," 242.
40. W. K. Fellows, letter to Gustav A. Andreen, January 19, 1926.
41. Fellows, letter to Andreen
42. Fellows, letter to Andreen.
43. Minutes of the WMS Executive Board, Chicago, February 13, 1923.
44. Jane Telleen, "Women's Missionary Society," 243.
45. Bergendoff, *Augustana . . . A Profession of Faith*, 156.
46. Bergendoff, 156
47. Hurty, "Emmy Carlsson Evald," 260.
48. Augustana College Special Collections, "An Augustana Campus History," accessed December 30, 2016, http://www.augustana.edu/SpecialCollections /CampusHistory/section2.html.

49. McCann, "For 40 Years Mrs. Emmy Evald Has Gone Building 'Round the World," *New York Sun*, March 2, 1932.
50. Evald, personal papers.
51. Mrs. C. R. Freedlund (article, n.p., n.d.).
52. Lani L. Johnson, *Led by the Spirit: A History of Lutheran Church Women* (Philadelphia: Lutheran Church Women, 1980), 5.
53. Jane Telleen, "Women's Missionary Society," 243.

Chapter Seven: Life at Berwyn Avenue (1930–1940)

1. Mumford, "Remembrances of Emmy Evald," 4.
2. Mumford, 4.
3. Mumford, 1.
4. Mumford, 2.
5. Mumford, 2.
6. Mumford, 5.
7. Robert W. Rydell, "Century of Progress Exposition," in *The Encyclopedia of Chicago* (Chicago: University of Chicago Press, 2004), 124–126.
8. Rydell, "Century of Progress Exposition," 125.
9. *The Immanuel Review* (October 1934), 2.
10. Carl A. Olson, secretary, Upsala College, letter to Emmy Evald, April 11, 1935.
11. Joshua Lindstrom, speech, reprinted in *Mission Tidings* (June 1935).
12. *The Newark Legend*, June 4, 1935.
13. Bengtson, "Doctor Emmy Evald" (speech).
14. Mary Ashby Cheek, letter to Evald Lawson, January 10, 1939.
15. Catherine Waugh McCulloch, letter to Mrs. Rutledge, n.d.
16. Jane Telleen, "'Yours in the Master's Service': Emmy Evald and the Woman's Missionary Society of the Augustana Lutheran Church, 1892–1942," *Swedish Pioneer Historical Quarterly* 30, no. 3 (July 1979): 192–193.
17. McCann, "A New Honor for Dr. Emmy Evald," *New York Sun*, (n.d.).
18. Mary Ashby Cheek, letter to Emmy Evald, December 12, 1938.
19. Catherine Waugh McCulloch, letter to "Friends of Emmy Evald," n.d.
20. Mary Ashby Cheek, letter to Catherine Waugh McCulloch, March 6, 1941.
21. Emmy Evald, letter to Mary Ashby Cheek, August 1, 1939.
22. *The Lutheran Companion* (February 23, 1939).

Chapter Eight: The Lutheran Home (1930–1935)

1. Elna Johanson, letter to Emmy Evald, May 15, 1931.
2. Benson, *Acorns Small*, 13.
3. Minutes of the WMS Executive Board, Chicago, n.d., 303.
4. Joanne Reitano, *The Restless City: A Short History of New York from Colonial Times to the Present* (New York: Routledge/Taylor and Francis Group, 2006), 133.
5. Reitano, 131–143.
6. Emmy Evald, Among Ourselves, *Mission Tidings* (n.d.).
7. Emmy Evald and Augusta O. Anseen, eds., *Tenth Anniversary Souvenir: 1931–1941* (New York: n.p., n.d.), 7–10.
8. Evald and Anseen, 9.
9. Johanson, letter to Emmy Evald, May 15, 1931.
10. *New York Times* (November 16, 1930).
11. Evald and Anseen, *Tenth Anniversary Souvenir*, 8.

12. Evald, Among Ourselves, *Mission Tidings* (n.d.).
13. Evald and Anseen, *Tenth Anniversary Souvenir*, 8.
14. Evald and Anseen, 9.
15. Minutes of the WMS Executive Board, Chicago, May 18, 1936, 2.
16. Evald and Anseen, *Tenth Anniversary Souvenir*, 7–10.
17. Evald and Anseen, 10.
18. Evald, personal papers.
19. Evald, Among Ourselves, *Mission Tidings* (n.d.).
20. Evald and Anseen, *Tenth Anniversary Souvenir*, 10.
21. Signe H. Stolpe, *A Tribute* (New York: n.p., June 1937).
22. Evald, Among Ourselves, *Mission Tidings* (n.d.).
23. Evald, Among Ourselves, *Mission Tidings* (n.d.).
24. Evald, Among Ourselves, *Mission Tidings* (n.d.).
25. Minutes of the WMS Executive Board, Chicago, September 6, 1930.
26. Minutes of the WMS Executive Board, Chicago, June 30, 1931.
27. Emmy Evald, Among Ourselves, *Mission Tidings*, no. 1 (July 1935), 28–29.
28. Bengtson, "Doctor Emmy Evald" (speech).
29. Lars E. Carlsson, e-mail message to author, April 22, 2005.
30. *Lutheran Home for Women* (brochure, n.p., n.d.).
31. Minutes of the WMS Executive Board, Chicago, September 28, 1933.
32. *Proceedings of the WMS 43rd Annual Conference* (Minneapolis, June 7–11, 1934), 277.
33. Minutes of the WMS Executive Board, Chicago, February 24, 1934.
34. Minutes of the WMS Executive Board, Chicago, September 9, 1935.
35. Evald and Anseen, *Tenth Anniversary Souvenir*, 22.
36. Emmy C. Carlson, "Characters I Have Known" (essay, Julia Richman High School, [1935?]).
37. Alana Erickson Coble, *Cleaning Up: The Transformation of Domestic Service in Twentieth Century New York City* (New York: Routledge/Taylor and Francis Group, 2006), 2–30, 73.
38. Coble, 2–30.
39. Coble, 3.
40. Evald, personal papers.
41. "Reception Tendered Dr. Emmy Evald by Emmy Evald Auxiliary," *Mission Tidings*, 32, no. 5 (November 1937): 137.
42. *Glimpses* (November 1937).
43. "A Colossal Birthday Celebration," *The Immanuel Review*, no. 10 (October 1937): 2.
44. Evald and Anseen, *Tenth Anniversary Souvenir*, 11.
45. Evald and Anseen, 47.
46. Evald and Anseen, 45.
47. Emmy Evald, letter to the WMS Executive Board, as printed in *Mission Tidings* (February 3, 1931).
48. Minutes of the WMS Executive Board, Chicago, November 11, 1935.

Chapter Nine: The Showdown (1935–1938)

1. Evald and Anseen, *Tenth Anniversary Souvenir*, 50.
2. Minutes of the WMS Executive Board, Chicago, September 9, 1935.
3. Minutes of the WMS Executive Board, Chicago, September 24, 1935.
4. Minutes, September 24, 1935.
5. Minutes of the WMS Executive Board, Chicago, October 14, 1935.
6. Minutes, October 14, 1935.

7. Minutes, October 14, 1935.
8. Minutes of the WMS Executive Board, Chicago, October 14, 1935.
9. Minutes of the WMS Executive Board, Chicago, December 14, 1936.
10. Minutes, December 14, 1936.
11. Minutes of the WMS Executive Board, Chicago, September 24, 1935.
12. Minutes, September 24, 1935.
13. Minutes of the WMS Executive Board, Chicago, April 7, 1936.
14. Minutes of the WMS Executive Board, Chicago, September 24, 1935.
15. Evald and Anseen, *Tenth Anniversary Souvenir*, 50.
16. Minutes of the WMS Executive Board, Chicago, February 26, 1938.
17. Evald and Anseen, *Tenth Anniversary Souvenir*, 50.
18. Minutes of the WMS Executive Board, Chicago, June 23, 1938.
19. Evald and Anseen, *Tenth Anniversary Souvenir*, 50.
20. Minutes of the WMS Executive Board, Chicago, July 11, 1938.
21. Minutes, July 11, 1938.
22. Minutes, July 11, 1938.
23. Minutes of the WMS Executive Board, Chicago, July 20, 1938.
24. Evald and Anseen, *Tenth Anniversary Souvenir*, 50.

Epilogue

1. Evald and Anseen, *Tenth Anniversary Souvenir*, 13.
2. Evald and Anseen, 13.
3. *Glimpses* (December 1942).
4. Rockford College Alumni Association, letter to Emmy Evald, September 12, 1942.
5. Mumford, "Remembrances of Emmy Evald," 6.
6. Mumford, 6
7. Evald and Anseen, *Tenth Anniversary Souvenir*, 11, 16.
8. Evald and Anseen, 11, 16.
9. "Dr. Evald Is Attending 50th Convention," *Jamestown Post-Journal*, June 9, 1942.
10. Evald and Anseen, *Tenth Anniversary Souvenir*, 14.
11. Evald and Anseen, 14.
12. *Immanuel Review*, no. 1 (January 1947).
13. Minutes from the WMS Executive Board, Chicago, February 5, 1947.
14. Bengtson, "Doctor Emmy Evald" (speech).
15. *Mission Tidings* (n.d.).
16. Benson, *Acorns Small*, 18.
17. Marion Lindquist, "WMS—A Journey Remembered," *Augustana Heritage Newsletter* 3, no. 3 (March 1998): 8.

About the Author

Since childhood, Sharon M. Wyman has heard family stories about Emmy Evald. They were grand tales indeed of Emmy's trip to China, where she thwarted a robbery attempt, and of her travels to India, where she spent the day with a viper in her cot. But it was not until Wyman relocated to Chicago, where Evald grew up, that her interest in family history blossomed.

As Evald's great-granddaughter, Wyman has access to her personal papers, scrapbooks, and photographs. Plus, she has the inside scoop from family members who knew Evald best, adding to an intimate portrait of Evald's life.

Wyman grew up in St. Louis, Missouri, and spent twenty years in corporate communications. She currently lives on Cape Cod with her husband, Bob, their beagle Annie, and a cat named Calvin.

sharonwyman.com

CPSIA information can be obtained
at www.ICGtesting.com
Printed in the USA
JSHW020253101122
32924JS00003B/181